What Are Children's Rights?

ISSUES FOR THE NINETIES

Volume 13

Editor

Craig Donnellan

Independence
Educational Publishers
Cambridge

First published by Independence
PO Box 295
Cambridge CB1 3XP

© Craig Donnellan 1996

British Library Cataloguing in Publication Data
What Are Children's Rights? – (Issues for the Nineties Series)
I. Donnellan, Craig II. Series
323.3'52

ISBN 1 872995 79 9

Printed in Great Britain
at Leicester Printers Ltd
Leicester, Great Britain

Typeset by
Claire Boyd

Cover
The illustration on the front cover is by
Andrew Smith / Folio Collective.

CONTENTS

Introduction

What Are Children's Rights is the thirteenth volume in the series: **Issues For The Nineties**. The aim of this series is to offer up-to-date information about important issues in our world.

What Are Children's Rights examines the legal aspects of children's rights, and the sensitive issues of child abuse and bullying. The information comes from a wide variety of sources and includes:

Government reports and statistics
Newspaper reports and features
Magazine articles and surveys
Literature from lobby groups
and charitable organisations.

It is hoped that, as you read about the many aspects of the issues explored in this book, you will critically evaluate the information presented. It is important that you decide whether you are being presented with facts or opinions. Does the writer give a biased or an unbiased report? If an opinion is being expressed, do you agree with the writer?

What Are Children's Rights offers a useful starting-point for those who need convenient access to information about the many issues involved. However, it is only a starting-point. At the back of the book is a list of organisations which you may want to contact for further information.

*****

The rights of the child

A guide to the UN Convention

Everyone has human rights, including children. Because they are young, however, children are more likely than adults to have their rights forgotten about or ignored. To protect children's rights the United Nations has drawn up an international agreement called the United Nations Convention on the Rights of the Child.

The Convention is an important step forward because, for the first time, all the rights of children have been written down in one document.

The UK Government agreed to be bound by the Convention in 1991. This means the Government has to make sure that our laws and the way we treat children in this country meet the standards laid down in the Convention.

What is the Convention?
What does it say?
The Convention sets out in a number of statements (called articles) the rights which all children and young people up to the age of 18 should have. The rights should apply to young people everywhere whether they live in rich or poor countries. The Convention says children have three main rights which must be considered whenever any decision is being made about them, or any action is taken which affects them.

Non-discrimination
All the rights in the Convention apply to all children equally whatever their race, sex, religion, language, disability, opinion or family background (Article 2).

Best interests
When adults or organisations make decisions which affect children they

must always think first about what would be best for the child (Article 3).

The child's views
Children too have the right to say what they think about anything which affects them. What they say must be listened to carefully. When courts or other official bodies are making decisions which affect children they must listen to what the children want and feel (Article 12).

What other rights does the Convention give children?
Civil and political rights
These are to do with children being respected as people and having a right to take part in society, and to be involved in matters which are important to them.

Name and nationality at birth
All children have a right to a name when they are born and to be able to become a citizen of a particular country (Article 7).

Freedom of expression
Children have the right to express what they think and feel so long as by doing so they do not break the law or affect other people's rights (Article 13).

Freedom of thought, conscience and religion
Parents have a duty to give guidance but children have the right to choose their own religion, and to have their own views as soon as they are able to decide for themselves (Article 14).

Meeting other people
Children have the right to join organisations and to take part in meetings, and peaceful demonstrations, so long as they are not against the law and that by doing so children do not affect other people's rights (Article 15).

Privacy
Children have the right to personal privacy. This includes not having their personal letters opened or anyone listening in to their personal phone calls unless the law allows this (Article 16).

Access to information
Children should be able to get hold of a wide range of information, especially any which would make life better for them (Article 17).

Protection from violence and harmful treatment
Children have the right to be protected from all forms of violence. They must be kept safe from harm. They must be given proper care by those looking after them (Article 19).

Children have a right not to be punished cruelly or in a way that would belittle them. They must not be locked up unless the law says they may be. When they are locked up lawfully they must be treated with respect. They must be able to have legal advice and to have their case heard and decided on as quickly as possible (Article 37).

Any child who has been badly treated must be given help to recover (Article 39).

Breaking the law
Children who get into trouble with the law must be treated in a way which is suited to their age. They are to be treated as innocent unless and until they are found guilty. They must be able to get legal advice and be represented by a lawyer. Wherever possible they should be dealt with other than through the courts. They should be sent to prison only when there is no other suitable sentence and then only for the shortest time possible (Articles 37 and 40).

Economic, social, cultural and protective rights

These cover the child's rights to proper standards of physical care, education, health and protection from harm.

Rights to life
Children have a right to life and to the best possible chance to develop fully (Article 6).

Standards of living
Every child has the right to an adequate standard of living. This is, in the main, for parents to provide, but in cases of need the Government should help parents reach this standard (Article 27). Every child has the right to benefit from social security taking account of the resources and circumstances of the child and those responsible for the child (Article 26).

Day-to-day care
The Convention says children should be cared for properly from day to day. This is mainly for the child's parents to do but the Government is expected to give suitable help to parents (Article 18).

If children cannot live with their family, they must be properly looked after by another family or in a children's home. The child's race, religion, culture and language must all be considered when a new home is being chosen for the child (Article 20).

Any child being looked after away from home in a boarding school, long-stay institution or hospital must also receive proper care (Article 3).

Children should be separated from their parents against their will only if it is in the child's best interests. If this has to happen, the child, their parents and anyone else entitled to have an interest has the right to go to court and ask to have their case heard (Article 9).

If separated from parents, the child has the right to keep in touch regularly with the parents, unless this would be harmful to the child (Article 9).

If a child is being adopted into a new family either from the same or another country, this must be in line with strict procedures, laid down in the law to make sure that what happens is in the best interest of the child (Article 21).

Governments must take steps to stop children being taken out of the country illegally (Article 11).

Health and health care
Children have the right to be as healthy as possible. If they are ill they must be given good health care to enable them to become well again. The Government must try to reduce the number of deaths in childhood and to make sure that women having babies are given good medical care (Article 24).

Disabled children
Disabled children must be helped to be as independent as possible and to be able to take a full and active part in everyday life (Article 23).

A healthy environment
Children have the right to live in a safe, healthy and unpolluted environment with good food and clean drinking water (Article 24).

Education
Every child has the right to free education up to primary school level at least. Different kinds of secondary school education should be available for children. For those with the ability, higher education should also be provided (Article 28).

Schools should help children develop their skills and personality fully, teach them about their own and other people's rights and prepare them for adult life (Article 29).

Leisure
Every child is entitled to rest and play and to have the chance to join in a wide range of activities (Article 31).

Protection from exploitation
The Government must protect children from:
- doing work which could be dangerous or which could harm their health or interfere with their education (Article 32);
- dangerous drugs (Article 33);
- sexual abuse (Article 34);
- being abducted or sold (Article 35).

Armed conflict
The Convention says children under 15 years old are not to be recruited into the armed forces. In recruiting among young people aged between 15 and 18, priority should be given to those who are oldest (Article 38).

The Government's commitment

The Government is committed to support the convention and to make it known to the public. In 1994 and every five years after that, it will send the UN Committee on the Rights of the Child a report explaining how it is putting the Convention into practice. The Government also recognises the importance of working together with poorer countries to make life better for children living there.

The Government has entered certain 'reservations'. This means it will not necessarily follow the Convention in every respect. One reservation is that the Government regards the Convention as applying only after a live birth. Others are about immigration and nationality; employment law affecting 16 to 18-year-olds and the separation of children from adults in prison.

How can you use the convention?

What you can do
You can check the treatment of children in this country against the standards set out in the Convention. If you believe a child is not being given the rights spelled out in the Convention, you can tell Government departments, MPs, local councillors or children's organisations.

You can also encourage people to discuss the Convention and the rights of children at home, at work, in schools and parents' organisations and try to persuade people in charge to build its principles into their work.
● This article was produced by the Department of Health in conjunction with the Children's Rights Development Unit.

The extent of violence involving children

The following is from a summary of the report of the Commission on Children and Violence convened by the Gulbenkian Foundation

Children are far more often victims of violence than perpetrators of violence, and certain groups of children, including disabled children and some ethnic groups, are particularly at risk. One of the most disturbing social statistics is that the risk of homicide for babies under the age of one is almost four times as great as for any other age-group. There is increasing knowledge of and sensitivity to violence to children – in particular to sexual abuse and to bullying and other violence in institutions; it is not possible to tell whether the incidence of these forms of violence has increased or become more visible. There are problems about building any accurate picture of violence to children within families, but the most recent UK research shows that a substantial minority of children suffer severe physical punishment; most children are hit by their parents, up to a third of younger children more than once a week.

Only a very small proportion of children – mostly male but with an increasing minority of young women – get involved in committing violent offences. Very roughly, four per 1,000 young people aged between 10 and 18 are cautioned or convicted for offences involving violence against the person.

In terms of trends it appears that children's involvement in some but not all crimes of violence in the UK has increased over the last decade. But in comparison with the USA, overall levels of interpersonal violence in the UK are very low, and there is recent evidence that in comparison with some European countries, levels of self-reported violence by children in the UK are also low.

Children and violence, the report of the Commission on Children and Violence, convened by the Gulbenkian Foundation, was published by the Foundation in November 1995. The report is available from Turnaround Distribution Ltd, 27 Horsell Road, London N5 1XL, price £10.95 plus £2 postage and packing. Payment should be made by cheque or postal order to Turnaround Distribution Ltd.
● A free summary is available from Calouste Gulbenkian Foundation, 98 Portland Place, London W1N 4ET.

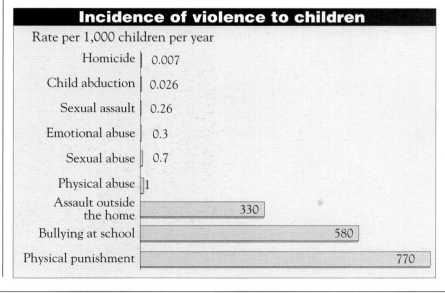

Incidence of violence to children

Rate per 1,000 children per year

Homicide	0.007
Child abduction	0.026
Sexual assault	0.26
Emotional abuse	0.3
Sexual abuse	0.7
Physical abuse	1
Assault outside the home	330
Bullying at school	580
Physical punishment	770

A guide to the Children Act – for parents

From the National Council for Family Proceedings

Introduction

The Children Act 1989 came into force on October 14th 1991. It made radical changes to the law about the upbringing of children. It affects all children and their families.

The Children Act is particularly important to families going through change when parents separate or divorce or when a parent dies. (The Children Act also provides protection for children at risk, but this is not dealt with here.)

Much of the old law is abolished. The new law emphasises that parents have responsibilities for children rather than rights over them. Courts are discouraged from making orders except where they are needed to benefit the child.

The Children Act has introduced a new set of orders which can deal with practical issues when they arise. 'Custody' and 'access' orders are no longer made. Children are given more right to be listened to in court proceedings about them.

What is parental responsibility?

Parental responsibility enables a person to take a decision about the child's upbringing, such as where the child should live and which school he or she should attend. Generally parental responsibility continues until a child is 18, although children can now make more decisions for themselves as they get older.

Parents keep their parental responsibility if they separate or if they divorce, even if they do not live with the child. A divorce brings a marriage to an end but not parenthood. Generally a parent only loses parental responsibility if a child is adopted by somebody else. The Children Act encourages parents who do not live with their children to remain in touch and to be involved in the child's life.

Under the old law when parents divorced, custody and access orders were usually made about the children. These orders gave the impression that one parent was being shut out from the child's life. Parents are now encouraged to make their own joint decisions and no orders will be made by a court unless needed.

Assistance is available from conciliation services, the Court Welfare Service, social services and solicitors to promote children's welfare by resolving disputes away from court. The Children Act recognises that courts should be a last resort for family decisions over children.

Who has parental responsibility?

Both parents have equal parental responsibility if they were married to each other when the child was born or marry each other afterwards.

If the parents of the child have never married each other only the mother initially has parental responsibility. The Children Act enables unmarried parents to make a formal agreement to share parental responsibility without going to court. A special form must be used to record this agreement and this must be registered with the court. If the parents cannot agree, the father can ask a court to give him parental responsibility.

Parents can ask somebody else, such as a relative or friend, to carry out their parental responsibility for them, for example, while they spend some time abroad or in hospital. Parents who do this remain responsible for their child.

People who are not parents, like step-parents, grandparents and other relatives, do not automatically have parental responsibility even though the child may be living with them. However, they may acquire parental responsibility in three ways. They may be appointed guardian by a parent with parental responsibility

(see below). They may obtain a Residence Order from a court (see below). Or, more rarely, they may adopt the child. A step-parent does not obtain parental responsibility simply by marrying the child's parent.

Even if people do not have parental responsibility for a child, the Act encourages them to do what is reasonable to look after the child while they have care of him or her. Adults who have temporary care of children, like childminders, teachers, babysitters, relatives and friends, also have to do what is reasonable to look after the child in their care.

Guardians

The Children Act makes it easier to appoint guardians to care for children if their parents die. This need no longer be made by way of a will but must be in writing, signed and dated.

A guardian is appointed to have parental responsibility on the death of a parent who had parental responsibility. A guardian's appointment will only take effect when both of the children's parents are dead unless the deceased parent had a Residence Order in his or her favour or was the only one with parental responsibility.

If a parent does not appoint a guardian before death a court may appoint one if needed.

When are court orders made?

Although courts are discouraged from making unnecessary orders, they are given more flexibility if an order is needed. Anyone who is genuinely concerned about a child can apply to court at any time and the court is given a new range of practical orders to make.

The orders should be able to deal with any question which arises in the child's life. Children themselves can apply for an order if they have sufficient understanding to do so.

The court will decide what is best for the child and will not make an order unless it is better for the child than not making an order.

The Children Act provides a checklist of factors which the court will consider in order to decide what is best for the child. At the top of the list are the child's wishes and feelings which will be assessed in the light of his/her age and understanding. Other factors in the checklist include the child's age, sex and background, his or her physical, emotional and educational needs and the ability of those concerned to meet those needs, and the likely effect on the child of a change of his or her circumstances. When a court is involved in a dispute the court will usually be informed of these factors through a Welfare Report.

Courts are required to set timetables to ensure that there is no unnecessary delay. They are expected to hear cases more quickly than in the past as delay is usually not in the child's interest.

What are the court orders?

– Residence Orders
– Contact Orders
– Specific Issue Orders
– Prohibited Steps Orders
– Family Assistance Orders

They each decide a particular question in a child's life

A *Residence Order* – decides with whom the child is to live. It does not remove the parental responsibility of the other parent. Residence Orders do affect some other matters, such as the change of the child's surname, the appointment of a guardian and when the child can be taken out of the United Kingdom.

(If you have an old Custody Order, it is not abolished by the Children Act. The Act does change the effect of an existing Custody Order in several respects, but does not convert the Custody Order into a Residence Order.)

A *Contact Order* – decides matters about the child's contact with any other person. It can deal with face-to-face meetings with the child and other forms of contact such as letters, telephone calls, cards and photographs. It is an order to the parent with whom the child lives to allow contact with the other parent.

Specific Issue and *Prohibited Steps Orders* – decide particular questions in a child's life, such as schooling, medical treatment or emigration.

A *Family Assistance Order* – where a family may need specialist help a Family Assistance Order can be made. This is a short-term order to a Court Welfare Officer or a Social Services Department to advise and assist a family for about six months. It can only be made with the consent of the adults involved and it is intended to help adults resolve those conflicts surrounding divorce or separation which affect children.

These new orders can be made in any proceedings about the family such as divorce, separation, maintenance, injunction or care proceedings. The Court has power to put conditions on any of the new orders, for example to specify exactly when a person should have contact with a child.

Children Act – a guide for children

The Children Act is the new law about the welfare of children. This information explains the new law where parents separate or divorce or where a parent dies. The main changes for children are:

- Parents have 'parental responsibility' for children rather than 'parental rights' over them. Generally this responsibility continues until the child is 18 although children can now make more decisions for themselves as they get older.
- The Act encourages parents and children to agree between themselves about children's arrangements rather than to go to court.
- Children who are old enough have the right to apply to court for orders about their upbringing.
- When making decisions about a child a court will always try to do what is best for that child.
- The court will take into account the child's wishes and feelings before making a decision.
- Courts are now expected to hear children's cases more quickly and to prevent delay which would be against the child's interests.

● The above is an extract from *A guide to the Children Act – for parents*, produced by the National Council for Family Proceedings.

Youth rights in Scotland

What are youth rights?

Under 16s

When you reach 18, the law treats you as an adult. Before that, you have some rights, but not others. It's important to know what rights you do have, to make sure adults take what you say SERIOUSLY and act on it.

Did you know that under 16s . . .

- Have a right to a doctor's appointment
- Can get a part-time job once they reach age 13
- Don't have to give any information to the police except their name and address
- Have a right to know if they are suspected of anything (by the police)
- Have a right to free legal advice from a lawyer

Where can you find out more?

The Scottish Child Law Centre is the only place in Scotland specialising in under 18s' rights. SCLC has five legally trained staff members how can advise you about your rights in general and tell you how the law affects you. We give advice by phone. We're based in Glasgow but cover the whole of Scotland.

If you call before 9am or after 5pm, or at weekends, you might get the answerphone.

Please leave your name and phone number (with the area code) and tell us the best time to call you back

Seeing a doctor

Under 16s have a legal right to see a doctor without a parent being with them. It is up to the doctor to decide whether you are mature enough to consent to treatment. The doctor might refuse to give you the treatment if s/he thinks you don't

fully understand, but should still respect your confidentiality – that is, your right to privacy. This means your parents should not normally be involved at all, unless you wish them to be involved.

Getting a job

You must be at least 13 to work, but, even if you are old enough, some jobs are outlawed. You can't work in quarries or the building trade, sell things 'door-to-door', or serve in pubs or betting shops.

You can't work during school hours, and not before 7am or after 7pm any day. You can only work for two hours on Sundays.

Babysitting

There is no set age at which you are allowed to babysit. If you are under 16, though, it is not advisable, since you are still legally a 'child' yourself, and the baby's parents will be responsible for your safety as well as the baby's. Ask yourself – Do I think I can handle any emergency, if it happens?

Parents splitting up?

If parents split up and can't agree on where you should live, or how often

you should see each of them, the court can make orders dealing with this. Judges should know what you think before they decide. Make sure that you have been asked your views. You could speak to the judge in person, if s/he agrees – this is up to the judge to decide. Some judges don't speak to children alone, others think it is a good idea. You could explain what you think to a person who has been asked to do a report for the court on what might be best. This person could be a social worker or a lawyer, and should put what you say into his or her report. If you have tried your best to explain to your parents and other adults involved what you want, but you feel no one is listening to you, it might help to have a lawyer of your own. (see *Getting free legal advice*).

You and the police

The police can stop you in the street. They should have a good reason to think you have witnessed a crime, or have committed a crime, before they stop you.

Apart from giving your name and address if asked for it, you don't need to answer any other questions, although there will be some situations where you will want to help the police with enquiries. If the police ask you to go to the police station, find out why they want you to go. If you are not being arrested, you are either being asked to go of your own free will – in which case you can refuse – or you are being 'detained'. Being 'detained' means being held for up to six hours, because the police suspect you have committed a crime. Make sure you know what they think you have done. If you are taken to a police station, ask the police about telling someone – like a parent – where you are. If you are arrested, ask for a lawyer.

The police have no automatic rights to search you, unless you have been arrested or 'detained'. They can search you if they have a good reason to think you have drugs, stolen property or a weapon on you.

Children's panels

Children's panels are where ordinary men and women, who have been trained to understand children's problems, decide what help should be given to a child and his/her family, to avoid the child getting into trouble, or to make sure the child is safe.

Usually only under-16s are sent to panels. A young person accused of a crime, or who has been taking drugs or alcohol, might go to a panel. If social workers suspect a child might be in danger at home – because of violence or sexual abuse – they could suggest that the child should go to a panel. Sometimes, children who are not going to school regularly also go to panels. The person who makes the final decision on who goes to a panel is the Reporter to the Children's Panel.

If you are going to a panel, remember: If you don't agree with why you have been brought to the panel, say so. If the reason is that you have allegedly committed a crime, then it is vital that you get legal advice before you go to a panel. Don't accept the statement about what you are supposed to have done unless you think it is right. You can appeal against any panel decision to a Sheriff.

You have a right to take someone with you to help you speak at a panel – this could be a relative or a friend.

The panel has the power to order that you and your family are given social-work support to help with problems at home. Sometimes, they may say a child needs to live with a new family for a while, or – in very difficult cases – that a young person should go to a children's home.

If you are in the care of a local authority, you will have special rights to have your views taken into account when decisions are being made about you. Phone the Scottish Child Law Centre to check what your rights in care are, or see a lawyer. You can get free legal advice (see below).

Getting free legal advice

Once you are 16, you always have a right to your own lawyer. Whether you are under or over 16, you will normally get free legal advice. The lawyer's fees are paid for you if you can't afford it and most young people will qualify.

In some situations, your parent will be your legal representative, while you are under 16. In other situations, you should be able to get a lawyer in your own right. This is not just when you've done something wrong. If what you want and what your parents want are totally different, it might be a good idea to have your own lawyer, for example, if your parents have agreed about where you have to live when they split up, but you have very good reasons for wanting to live somewhere else. You could also get your own lawyer if there is no one who can act for you – for example, if you live away from home, with someone who is not a parent, for example, an aunt, grandparent, foster parent, etc.

Under 18s
Free confidential legal advice
0800 317 500 –
The Scottish Child Law Centre is an organisation which gives advice, information and commentary on child law and children's rights for the benefit of under-18s in Scotland.

Freephone for young people:
Tel: 0800 317 500
(9am – 5pm Monday to Friday).

Advice line for adults:
Tel: 0141 226 3737
(10am – 4pm Tuesday to Friday)

Business line (to order publications, get information about training, etc.):
Tel: 0141 226 3434
Fax: 0141 226 3043

Write to us at:
Scottish Child Law Centre
Cranston House
108 Argyle Street
Glasgow G2 8BH

● IMPORTANT: Readers should note that the law in England and Wales is different to that in Scotland.

© *Scottish Child Law Centre*
1995

At what age can I . . .?

From the Children's Legal Centre

At fourteen

– You have full criminal responsibility for your actions in the same way that an adult has.

– If you are convicted of a criminal offence and break your promise to be bound over to keep the peace and be of good behaviour, you can be fined up to £1000.

– If you are convicted of a criminal offence you can be fined by the Youth Court up to a maximum of £1000.

– If you are convicted of a criminal offence, you can receive an Attendance Centre Order requiring you to attend a Centre for a minimum of 12 hours.

– You can drive or ride an agricultural tractor or machine .

– If local by-laws allow, you can work for your parents on a week-day as a street trader.

– You can ride a horse on a road without wearing protective headgear.

– You may be granted a justices' licence to take part in public performances abroad.

– You can possess a shotgun or air weapon or ammunition. Under 14 you cannot have one in your possession unless you are supervised by someone over 21 or are using it at a rifle club or shooting gallery. You cannot have an assembled shotgun unless you are supervised by a person of 21 or unless it is securely fastened so it cannot be fired.

– You can enter a bar but you can only buy soft drinks. It is a criminal offence to buy, attempt to buy or drink alcohol in licensed premises and you may be fined up to £1000.

At fifteen

– You can see a category-15 film at the cinema.

– You can rent or buy a category 15 video.

– If you receive a custodial sentence, you can be detained in a young offender institution. You cannot be sent to prison until you are 21.

At sixteen

– You can leave school. The two school-leaving dates are at the end of the spring term and the Friday before the last Monday in May as amended by Education Act 1976.

– You are entitled to receive full-time education until you are 19. Schools, sixth-form colleges and city technology colleges are free.

– You can work full-time if you have left school, although there are some restrictions on the work you can do. For example you cannot work in a betting shop or in a bar during opening hours.

– You can get a National Insurance number.

– You may receive Income Support in certain circumstances. For example, if you are still in full-time education at school or college and are forced to live away from your parents and they are not keeping you, or you cannot work or take up a youth training place because you are disabled or have dependent children. You may also be able to obtain a discretionary payment of Income Support to avoid 'severe hardship'. Factors to be taken into account include your health and vulnerability and whether you have friends or relatives willing to accommodate or support you.

– You have to pay prescription charges, unless you are in full-time education, pregnant, in receipt of Income Support or Family Credit, on a low income or in certain other circumstances. You have to pay for a sight test and for glasses unless you are in full-time education, or your eyesight is constantly changing. You also have to pay for certain dental treatment if you are not in full-time education.

– You can probably leave home without the consent of your parents or anyone else with parental responsibility. Any Residence Order comes to an end at 16 and can only be extended in exceptional circumstances. Wardship proceedings could be brought by your parents for your return home, but the court is unlikely to force you home against your wishes. Where there are serious concerns for your welfare any person could apply for an emergency protection order or the police could place you in police protection. If you are under 17, Social Services could apply for a care order. It is unlikely that you would be forced to go home in any of those circumstances.

– You may be able to enter into a contract for housing since this is a 'necessary' and the landlord would be able to sue for rent. However, under-18s cannot hold an estate in land, and therefore cannot be granted a lease or tenancy although you could be granted a licence.

– If you are homeless, the housing authority has a duty to house you if you are homeless, in priority need and did not make yourself intentionally homeless. You may be a priority need, for example, if you are pregnant, have a child or can establish that you are vulnerable. The social services department also has a duty to provide you with accommodation if you are in need and your welfare is likely to be 'seriously prejudiced'. You can refuse to be removed from local authority accommodation by your parents or anyone else with parental responsibility.

– A girl can consent to heterosexual intercourse. Although a girl will not commit a criminal offence if she has sexual intercourse below this age, a boy aged 10 can be convicted of a criminal offence although if he is under the age of 14 the prosecution must prove that at the time of the offence he knew that what he was doing was seriously wrong.

– You can marry with parental consent. You'll need the consent of both parents if they are married or your father has parental responsibility where they are not married. Where your parents are separated you will only need consent of the parent who has a Residence Order. If parental consent is refused, a court may authorise the marriage. Alternatively you could get married in Scotland.

– You can join most trade unions at 16; you can join some unions if you are under 16.

– You can consent to surgical, medical or dental treatment, including the taking of blood samples and also choose your own doctor.

– Subject to specified circumstances, you have the right to apply for access to your health records – including those of a doctor, dentist, nurse, optician, child psychologist or psychotherapist.

– Subject to certain exceptions, you are entitled to apply for access to your school records which includes information from teachers, education social welfare officers and other education support staff. Your parents are also entitled to this information. Parents have the right of access in relation to under-16s.

– You can apply for your own passport (you will be deleted from a parent's passport at 16) but one parent must give written consent. You do not need a parent's consent if you are married or in the armed forces. Below 16, a parent or someone acting in loco parentis can apply for a separate passport for you.

– You can apply for 'green form' legal advice and assistance (this does not cover representation in court) and criminal legal aid and will be assessed on your own means.

– You have a right to an offer of a Youth Training (YT) place if you are not in work or full-time education.

– If you are convicted of a criminal offence, depending on the seriousness of the offence, the Youth Court can make a probation order over you for up to three years.

– If you are convicted of an imprisonable offence and you give your consent, the Youth Court can make a community service order requiring you to perform unpaid work in the community for between 40 and 240 hours.

– If you are convicted of an imprisonable offence, you can be given a probation order, placing you on probation for between one and three years and requiring you to perform community service between 40 and 100 hours.

– A boy can join the armed forces with parental consent.

– You can hold a licence to drive an invalid carriage or a moped.

– You can buy cigarettes, tobacco and cigarette papers. A young person can smoke at any age, but if you are under 16 and caught by a uniformed police officer or park-keeper, they can seize your tobacco and cigarette papers, but not your pipe or tobacco pouch.

– You can have beer, cider or wine with a meal in the restaurant or other room used for meals in a pub or hotel.

– You can buy liqueur chocolates.

– You can buy fireworks.

– You have to pay full fare on trains and on buses and tubes in London.

You might have to pay full fare in other areas.

– You may become a street trader.

– You can be trained to take part in dangerous performances without a local authority licence.

– You can sell scrap metal.

– You are allowed to enter or live in a brothel. (You are also allowed to do this under the age of four).

– You can be used by another person in order to beg in the street or any premises.

– You can act as a pilot-in-command of a glider.

At seventeen

– A care order can no longer be made on you.

– You can hold a licence to drive most vehicles apart from medium and heavy goods vehicles.

– You can buy any firearm or ammunition.

– If you have been charged with an offence and not granted bail, and are 17 but under 21, you will be sent to a remand centre.

– A girl can join the armed forces with parental consent.

– You can apply for a helicopter pilot's licence.

– You can buy or hire a crossbow. Under-17s who have in their possession a crossbow capable of discharging a bolt can be convicted of a criminal offence unless under the supervision of someone aged 21.

– You can be interviewed by the police without an appropriate adult being present.

• The above is an extract from the information sheet At what age can I... ?, covering the ages 5 to 21, produced by the Children's Legal Centre. See page 39 for address details.   ©Children's Legal Centre
January, 1996

DAD – AT WHAT AGE CAN I BE TAKEN SERIOUSLY?

KenPyne

If you care about children...

A guide to understanding child abuse

What is child abuse?

An estimated 150 to 200 children die in England and Wales every year following incidents of abuse or neglect. Thousands more suffer long-term emotional and psychological problems because of ill-treatment by their own parents or those looking after them.

There are four main types of abuse, though a child may experience more than one kind of abuse at any one time in his or her life. For example the child may be both physically and emotionally abused.

Physical abuse

Physical abuse is when parents or adults deliberately inflict injuries on a child or, knowingly, do not prevent them. It includes hitting, shaking, squeezing, burning or biting. It also includes using excessive force when feeding, changing or handling a child. Giving a child poisonous substances, inappropriate drugs or alcohol, and attempting to suffocate or drown a child are also examples of physical abuse.

Physical abuse can cause injuries including bruising, burns, fractures, internal injuries and brain damage. In the most extreme cases, physical abuse can cause death.

Emotional abuse

Emotional abuse is when parents continuously fail to show their child love or affection, or when they threaten, taunt or shout at a child, causing him or her to lose confidence and self-esteem, and to become nervous or withdrawn.

Emotional abuse hurts children very deeply. Children need love, reassurance and praise from their parents so that they can feel confident and happy in themselves.

When adults are constantly threatening, angry, sarcastic or critical they can make children feel unloved and unlovable. This can have serious effects on the child's personality and make it very hard for the child to form successful relationships as he or she grows up.

Neglect

Neglect occurs when parents fail to meet their child's essential needs, such as adequate food, clothing, warmth and medical care. Leaving children who are too young to look after themselves alone or without proper supervision is also an example of neglect.

Children who are neglected usually show signs of being unhappy in some way. They may appear withdrawn or unusually aggressive, or they may have lingering health problems or difficulties at school.

Sexual abuse

Sexual abuse takes place when an adult forces a child to take part in a

Photo: Sandra Lousada / NSPCC. Posed by model.

sexual activity, using the child to satisfy his or her own sexual desires. This can involve sexual intercourse, fondling, masturbation, oral sex, anal intercourse or exposing children to pornographic videos, books, magazines or other material.

Sexual abuse can have very damaging, and long-lasting effects. Studies have shown that sexually abused children may become abusers themselves, or may get involved in personal relationships which involve violence or abuse.

Why do adults abuse children?

No one knows exactly why some adults abuse children. There may be many different reasons. Stress, problems, unhappy circumstances, the feeling of having no power in adult relationships, and having been abused as a child may all play a part. But it is hard to predict with certainty which factors cause an adult to abuse a child.

Some adults may convince themselves that there is nothing wrong with their behaviour, or that it is for the child's own good.

But whatever the reason, abuse is always wrong, and it is never the child's fault.

It isn't only adults who abuse children. Sometimes older children abuse younger ones. It is very important that this is stopped as soon as it is discovered, for the sake of both the victim and the abuser, for whom it could become a dangerous habit.

● The above is an extract from the leaflet, *If you care about children – A guide to understanding child abuse*, produced by the NSPCC. See page 39 for address details.

© NSPCC

ChildLine logs 20,000 pleas for help a year

**By Celia Hall,
Medical Editor**

More than 20,000 children a year tell ChildLine that they have been sexually or physically abused, according to a report from the charity helpline published today.

Another 1,300 spoke of fear, neglect or threats made to them. While the majority of calls are about family problems, bullying, pregnancy, drug abuse or running away, one child in four is in danger from assault in some form, says ChildLine.

Mary MacLeod, policy director of ChildLine, who wrote the report, found that verbal abuse, alone or accompanying assault, was another feature of the calls.

The children were routinely sworn at, called all the forms of insults used in the adult world.

'But children are also told by their parents that they wished they were dead, had never been born. In the children's view this can be as bad as, and sometimes worse than, the physical assaults,' she said. One child was told: 'I'm going to dig a grave and put you in it.'

Most children were abused by parents or family members or friends of the family and, for most children, the abuse had been going on for months or years

The charity, set up in 1986, listens to 3,000 children on its telephone lines every day. British Telecom says that 10,000 attempts are made to get through on the 0800 1111 number every 24 hours.

Today's report forms Child-Line's evidence to the National Commission of Inquiry into the Prevention of Child Abuse, an independent investigation set up by the National Society for the Prevention of Cruelty to Children.

Miss MacLeod said: 'The sadistic abuse that children described to us is shocking but so is the lack of love and the constant fear that form the background to these children's lives.'

She said that children were terrified into silence by abusing adults, some were sent to school with sick notes to miss PE so that injuries would not be discovered.

The report says that in 1993-94 there were 10,942 sexual abuse calls, 10,028 physical abuse calls, 495 emotional abuse calls, 181 calls about neglect and 634 about fears of abuse.

Children who complained of sexual abuse told how the assaults were often engineered out of normal family behaviour, tickling, teasing, chase games, cuddling, having a bath, helping with homework or going to bed.

An 11-year-old said of her father: 'It happens when I come home from school. Mum doesn't know. I feel desperate. I hate him.'

ChildLine counselled 9,048 girls and 1,899 boys about sexual abuse in the year. In 94 per cent of cases it was by a person the child knew; 56 per cent were in the immediate family. Fathers were the abuser in 32 per cent of cases with girls and 30 per cent with boys.

Counsellors identified 11 calls in which children, usually girls, talked about organised abuse, including prostitution, and five which involved ritual abuse.

'Callers who describe being abused in bizarre circumstances with details which suggest sadistic rituals also display a level of terror of intervention which makes it difficult to amass evidence compelling enough to persuade sceptics of the existence of ritual abuse,' it says.

● *What children tell ChildLine about being abused*, £3; ChildLine, Royal Mail Building, Studd Street, London N1 0QW

*© The Telegraph
November, 1995*

Child protection in Scotland

Telling about child abuse and what happens next

The information which follows gives you a general idea of what you can expect if you are worried that a child in Scotland might be neglected or abused and you decide you would like to tell somone.

This information gives guidance about this very difficult situation. What happens can vary depending on where you live and the nature of the case. But what follows gives a general idea of what to expect.

Should you tell?

Yes, always. If you think that a child is being harmed you should tell whether you are a parent or relative, friend, teacher or neighbour. If you want to talk to someone about such a situation you should not feel worried or guilty at passing on any information.

Must you be certain that the child is being harmed?

Not necessarily. A person may know that a child is being left alone in the house but more often they 'have a feeling', a suspicion that something is wrong. A happy child may have become withdrawn; you may hear a youngster continually crying; you may have noticed a child having more bruises than seems normal. Or someone may have said something that worries you. If a child has suggested to you that something is happening to him or her, then encourage the child to talk to someone who can help. Remember that children rarely lie when talking about harm done to them so they should be taken seriously. Explain to them that there is no need to feel ashamed or guilty and that there is a lot of help available to sort out their problems.

Who should you tell?

It is the social work department's

Scottish Child Law Centre

responsibility to investigate child abuse, but you can tell anyone who is concerned about children, for example the RSSPCC or the Reporter to the Children's Panel as well as a social worker. You may find it easier to talk to someone you know like, your health visitor, your GP, a teacher at the local school or the local police officer. Whoever you tell, the welfare of the child will be their major concern.

If you do tell, what happens next?

Generally an immediate check is made to see whether the child or his or her family are already known to any of the people mentioned above, the social work department, the RSSPCC etc. These people may meet together to discuss the information you have passed on. If necessary, they can meet within hours of you speaking to someone. In other cases they may get together after an initial investigation has been made.

Is there always an investigation?

'Investigation' sounds a threatening word. What will happen will depend on the circumstances, but all information received is treated seriously and will be investigated. A social worker or health visitor may visit the family and find, for example, a single parent with a difficult child is needing help. Some support, such as help finding a nursery place, may be all that is needed to avoid a child coming to harm. If this is the case, then no further action may be needed. It could be that because you told someone of your worries, you prevent a child suffering. In other cases the first enquiries are made by social workers and the police acting together, particularly if it is suspected that a crime may have been committed against a child. Whatever the circumstances, the main concern of any investigating officer is always the welfare of the child.

Will you have to be interviewed?

Probably. Perhaps you can tell little more than you first reported. But if you have witnessed harm or neglect of a child, then your information may be crucial. Any help you can give in protecting a child will be appreciated by all those involved. If at the end of the day your fears for the child were groundless, that does not matter. You would still have been right to report your concern.

Will the child be removed from home?

Only when the child cannot be protected at home. In most cases the child will be able to stay at home. If a member of the household is involved then steps can be taken to remove that person from the home so that the child can stay put. If it is necessary to remove the child he or she may be taken to stay with relatives, or to a foster home or sometimes to a hospital. This may only be for a short time.

Will anyone else be involved?

If it is thought that a child may have been harmed or neglected, then the Reporter to the Children's Panel will be told and all the information will be passed to him. The Reporter may also attend any meetings to discuss the situation and will decide whether any action is needed to protect the child.

What action might the Reporter take?

The Reporter can decide to take no action, or can arrange for informal support for the family through, for example, a social worker visiting with the family's agreement. If the Reporter thinks it is necessary, he may refer the child to a Children's Hearing. If the Hearing thinks the child needs legal protection, they may allow the child to stay at home but insist that a social worker visits regularly. The Hearing may decide that the child should live somewhere else, perhaps with foster parents or relatives, or in a children's home or other place. The Children's Hearing will regularly look at the case to see whether the child can be returned home.

What happens to a person who harms a child?

Very often when a parent harms a child he or she has been coping with problems, perhaps money worries, or a violent relationship. Social-work help could ease the situation and make life better for the child and the family. But in some cases where there is sufficient evidence the person who has harmed the child may be prosecuted, and in the most serious cases the person could be imprisoned.

● IMPORTANT: Readers should note that the system for protecting children in Scotland is very different to that in England and Wales. A children's hearing system is involved in Scotland and there is a new law, the Children's (Scotland) Act 1995, which deals with this. For further information from the Scottish Child Law Centre, see page 39 for address details.   © Scottish Child Law Centre

Children's problems

From the ChildLine Annual Report, 1995

Calls and letters (1st April 1994 to 31st March 1995)

Type of problem	Girls	Boys	Total	%
Bullying	10,009	2,856	12,865	14

(This includes not only children who called the main 0800 1111 number about bullying but also 3,737 children counselled on a special national bullying line operated by ChildLine in 1994 with funding from a number of bodies, as part of a six-month anti-bullying campaign with the BBC Social Action Unit, and also 862 counselled on the Tayside Bullying Line operated by ChildLine Scotland for Tayside Council.)

Type of problem	Girls	Boys	Total	%
Family relationship problem	9,238	1,850	11,088	13
Physical abuse	6,703	2,896	9,599	11
Sexual abuse	7,459	1,748	9,207	10
Worries about others	8,356	860	9,216	10
Pregnancy	7,197	322	7,519	8
Partner relationship	3,098	315	3,413	4
Problem with friends	3,630	308	3,938	4
Sexuality	2,652	1,262	3,914	4
Facts of life	1,848	270	2,118	2
School problem	1,025	361	1,386	2
Runaway	973	515	1,488	2
Other*	10,228	2,736	12,964	14
Total	73,695	16,505	90,200	100

Photo: Posed by model. Larry Bray / ChildLine

* This breakdown refers to children calling or writing to ChildLine for the first time in 1994/95. It does not include those ongoing callers who first called ChildLine the previous year, nor does it include adults who sought our help. It is based on calls to both the main 0800 1111 service and all other special lines.

● The above is an extract from ChildLine's Annual Report, 1995. See page 39 for address details.

© ChildLine, 1995

Fact or fiction?

Like most people, you have probably heard or read a lot of stories about child abuse in the news lately. But how much do you really know about it? Test yourself on this quiz.

Decide which of the statements printed in bold are true and which are false. But try to make up your mind before reading the answers! Why not ask your partner or friend to do the quiz too, and compare your answers?

If a child is abused it won't make a lot of difference in the long run, as they won't remember much about it when they grow up.

False. Abuse can ruin a child's life. Younger children are likely to remember less about the experience, but the emotional and psychological effects may be even more damaging.

Children who have been abused may grow up feeling that they are worthless and may have difficulty forming happy relationships. Research has shown that they may also be more likely to turn to alcohol, drugs or crime, and may be more likely to abuse their own children.

It's not only poor parents from deprived backgrounds who abuse their children.

True. People who abuse children come from all social backgrounds, all walks of life, and different races and cultures. They can be parents, or other people the child knows well, like a family friend or close relative. (Only in one in every six or seven cases is the abuser a total stranger.)

'A good hiding never did anyone any harm.'

False. Adults who were physically punished when they were children sometimes say that it didn't do them any harm. But although we may not realise the connection between a bad experience in our childhood and the feelings and difficulties we may have as adults, the connection will almost certainly be there.

Child abuse is very rare. It's just the press that blows the problem out of all proportion.

False. No one knows exactly how common child abuse is, but the number of cases reported and the number of children receiving help are increasing every year. The NSPCC estimates that between 150 and 200 children die every year in England and Wales following incidents of abuse or neglect. Many incidents of abuse are never reported, but we know that three to four children die each week following abuse and neglect. The media have helped to make people aware of the problem, and this may be one reason why more cases of child abuse are being reported.

It is all right for fathers to hug and kiss their children – boys as well as girls – and for them to bath children too young to bath themselves.

True. All the news about sexual abuse cases recently has made some fathers worried about showing affection for their children. All these activities are perfectly normal and healthy. Children need to be shown warmth and affection by their fathers as well as their mothers.

It is only sexual abuse if a parent uses a child to satisfy his or her own sexual desires.

It is illegal for children under 13 to be left alone at home, for example, while their parents go out for the evening.

False. There is no law which states the age at which children can be left unsupervised. But parents can be prosecuted for neglect if they leave children who are too young to look after themselves and something happens to the child in their absence. Ideally, all babysitters should be 16 or over, because children under 16 cannot be held legally responsible for anything that happens to a child in their care.

Always try to make sure that your babysitter or child-minder is reliable and trustworthy, and listen to your instincts if you have any doubts about the person.

Smacking is not the best way to discipline a child.

True. Children need limits to be set to their behaviour, but punishing them with angry or aggressive actions is not the most effective way of doing this. It may not even make the child behave any differently and will not teach them respect or self-control. It is better to find positive ways of setting limits. For example, if children are used to love and praise, they will be upset by your disappointment and unsmiling face. With younger children you can usually distract their attention to something else.

Shouting at your children can't possibly be a form of child abuse.

False. You may well need to shout at a child sometimes – particularly if they are in immediate danger. But if you are constantly shouting and criticising, a child will feel unloved, and will feel that they can 'never do anything right'. Eventually they may have become withdrawn or develop other long-term behaviour problems.

● The above is an extract from the leaflet *If you care about children – A guide to understanding child abuse*, produced by the NSPCC. See page 39 for address details.

© NSPCC

ChildLine speaks out

'Unseen, unheard casualties of abuse live out their childhoods in misery'

A bleak picture of the cruelty and misery which thousands of children still suffer emerges from evidence given by ChildLine to the National Commission of Inquiry into the Prevention of Child Abuse and made public today (Monday, November 13, 1995).

One in four of the children who call the national free helpline for children in trouble or danger still do so because they are being physically or sexually abused – usually by someone they know, especially members of their own families. Most have been suffering the abuse for months, or even years.

ChildLine chairman Esther Rantzen commented; 'These are the unseen, unheard casualties of abuse, living their childhoods in misery. ChildLine helps children who feel they have nowhere else to turn, children who have been terrified into silence by their abusers, with threats of what will happen if they do speak out.

'Usually they are too frightened to say who they are and where they are calling from, or to ask ChildLine to alert police and social services – they just want to be able to pour out their troubles, often for the very first time, and are desperate for their abuse to stop. ChildLine counsellors reassure them that they have a right to be safe and try to help them to identify an adult they trust in whom they can confide.

'There are, alas, often no quick and easy solutions to the horrendous problems that children bring to ChildLine. But children tell us that just knowing that we are there, 24 hours a day, ready to listen to them, helps them to keep sane.'

Sexual abuse

Of the 10,942 children who called ChildLine about sexual abuse in 1993/94, 96 per cent were abused by someone they knew – 56 per cent by parents, brothers or sisters; others mainly by other relatives, neighbours or friends. Of those abused within the immediate family, 78 per cent were abused by their father or a father-figure (such as a stepfather or mother's boyfriend), usually when mothers were out. But some were also abused while other members of the family were in the house, asleep. Four per cent were abused by mothers (91 girls and 394 boys) and one per cent (33 girls and 48 boys) by both parents together.

One man who sexually abused his 13-year-old stepdaughter told her: 'It's only natural.'

'What appears casual, routine or ordinary to the abuser profoundly disturbs the child,' says Mary MacLeod, ChildLine's director of policy, research and information, who compiled ChildLine's evidence to the Commission.

While a few children describe one-off sexual assaults – mainly committed by someone outside the family – usually callers describe regular assaults occurring over periods of months or years.

Some sexually abused children describe violent and sudden assaults which shock and traumatise them, such as being woken and raped. Some are made to watch pornography and copy what they see. Others describe being photographed and videoed while being abused. Some talk of being threatened and beaten and others talk about being prostituted to parents' and brothers' friends.

Physical abuse

Eighty-nine per cent of the 10,028 children who called about physical abuse said they were physically assaulted by parents, brothers and sisters, with fathers responsible in 43 per cent of cases and mothers in 23 per cent. Boys are almost twice as likely as girls to report physical abuse by fathers.

Child callers describe 'smacks, slaps, pinches, squeezes, punches, kicks; being kicked out, across the room, downstairs; being thrown about, thrown downstairs or at walls or wardrobes; being scratched, bitten, shaken, crushed, strangled; being locked in rooms and cupboards, having toys broken, their things torn, their rooms wrecked.

'It is difficult to know from our contacts with children the extent of injuries. But most children talk about assaults which mark them: bruises, nose-bleeds, black eyes and belt marks, broken limbs, and some describe being given notes to excuse them from PE and games to avoid teachers seeing the evidence,' says Mary MacLeod.

Some children say that they are being punished for something that they have done but complain that the punishment is out of all proportion to the offence. Others live in a violent world where sudden outbursts of violence happen unpredictably and terrifyingly.

Lack of love and constant fear
'The sadistic abuse that the children describe to us is shocking,' says Mary MacLeod. 'But so are the lack of love and the constant fear that form the background to these children's lives.

'Children desperately want the abuse to stop but don't know how to achieve this. Some feel hopeless about anything changing in their lives. Some say they have tried to kill themselves or have run away. Some fantasise about killing a parent, or their abuser suddenly turning into a good parent.

'Children find it very hard to tell adults what is being done to them. Their abusers often terrify them into silence with threats of what they will do to them or to someone they love if they speak out. Or they tell children that no one will believe them. Sadly, if children do confide in an adult, they often find that they are greeted with incredulity by the very people who should be helping them.'

Remarkably, says Mary MacLeod, despite everything, many of ChildLine's callers still love their families and don't want to be taken away from them – they simply want the abuse to stop.

Photo: Larry Bray / ChildLine. Posed by model.

The causes of abuse
Why do parents abuse their children? Children often talk of family stress and parents' alcohol problems leading to physical violence and speak of parents 'taking things out' on them, says ChildLine. But children are shocked and baffled by sexual abuse and find it hard to believe what is happening to them, or to understand why. Sometimes, judging by what children tell ChildLine, it seems to be linked with 'serious emotional disorder' within a family. Sometimes there is a pattern of the boys and men in a family maltreating children.

Confidential help for mothers needed
Calls received by ChildLine mainly from mothers who discover that their child has been abused show that they, too, are terrified of reporting abuse by a member of their own family and, for some who live in closed or small communities, the public shame involved is too much to face. There is a pressing need for confidential help for mothers in these circumstances, argues Mary MacLeod. 'They are deeply shocked and need emotional support and thinking time. If they receive support, it is much more likely that they can give their children the protection and love that they so desperately need.'

It can be particularly hard for a non-abusing parent to intervene if parents are separated. 'The child's experience can be used as a football between parents and parents; lawyers seem to assume that an allegation of abuse is likely to be seen as malicious. They therefore often advise their clients to hold back.'

Court system can fail children
In the few cases where abusers are prosecuted, the court system tends to fail children, says ChildLine. Children may not receive the therapy or counselling that they need, for fear of 'contaminating' the evidence, and are banned from talking about the abuse outside their video interview. The Court Witness Pack published by ChildLine and NSPCC to help children to understand what will happen in court is often not provided.

ChildLine also says that when it refers cases of abuse to the police and social services, the response is 'variable'. While many offer immediate and sympathetic protection, 'some emergency duty teams seem very burdened and reluctant to respond'.

© ChildLine
November, 1995

Victims of violent crime

How to claim compensation

Have you been injured by violent crime? You may be able to claim compensation:

- The criminal need neither have been identified, nor prosecuted nor convicted
- The injury can be psychological, not just physical
- Claims can sometimes be successful years after the event.

This article gives information about how to claim from the new Criminal Injuries Compensation Authority under the '1996 Scheme'. This is a government scheme for compensating victims of violent crime. It deals with all claims made after 1st April 1986.

Who can claim?

Anyone injured by a violent crime can claim compensation – whether injured physically or psychologically. Generally, compensation is payable for injuries for which medical or other professional treatment (e.g. counselling) could be obtained.

This might be:

- a broken nose or scarring from an assault
- nervous shock from obscene or threatening telephone calls
- emotional trauma from sexual assault or rape, or witnessing a violent crime against a close relative.

You may also be able to claim where a close relative of yours has died as a result of the crime.

Compensation is not however available for:

- injuries resulting from road traffic crimes – for example, reckless driving – but get advice here
- Accidents – unless it happened whilst you were trying to prevent a crime or to escape from a criminal act

Photo: Larry Bray / ChildLine. Posed by model

- injuries sustained while committing a crime yourself
- very minor injuries.

When should I claim? . .

A new two year time limit:

The sooner the better: claims should normally be made not more than two years from the date of the crime, but the time limit can be waived in any case if the CICA think it reasonable and in the interests of justice to do so.

These might be because:

- you had repressed memories of a sexual assault
- you suffer from mental health problems – whether caused by the crime of violence or not
- the injury only became noticeable more than two years after the event – for example, brain damage.

but probably not:

- because you didn't know about the Criminal Injuries Compensation Scheme.

If you are 'time barred' it's often still well worth claiming (as soon as possible) – but get expert advise first.

What's it worth?

There's a tariff which tells you how much a particular injury is 'worth'. For example:

- multiple minor injuries £1,500
- dislocated jaw £2,000
- fractured skull (no operation) £2,500
- moderate brain damage £15,000

If you have more than one injury, you can claim the full tariff for the worst injury, but only 10% of the next most severe and 5% for the third.

So it's very important to claim for all your injuries and to make sure they are properly described when you apply.

Case study

Joe is attacked outside a pub and badly beaten up, suffering from a cracked skull, broken jaw, cuts bruises and a bloody nose. Some months later, friends and family begin to notice changes in Joe – he loses his job, starts sleeping rough, and becomes introspective and morose instead of cheerful and outgoing. A claim for his fractured skull is worth £2,500. His claim may be worth more however: £15,000 (moderate brain damage) + (10% of £2,500: fractured skull) + (5% of £2000: dislocated jaw) + (10% of £1,000: multiple minor injuries) = £15,350.

However, you may get less than the tariff, or nothing at all, if you:

- have a criminal record (probably but this is complicated)
- didn't help the police to prosecute the offender
- contributed to your own injury – for example by provoking an assault.

Don't be too put off by these limitations: when in doubt – apply!

What about the criminal?

You can get compensation even if the offender has not been identified far less convicted, or even charged. But you are expected to have reported the crime to the police immediately and help to prosecute the offender. If there are good reasons why you didn't report a crime or delayed to do so, get expert advise before making a claim.

Domestic violence

If you were injured as a result of domestic violence, you can still claim, but you will need to show that:

- the offender has been prosecuted, or that there were good reasons why not (for example, lack of evidence)

- you and the offender have permanently stopped living together at the time you made the claim (if you are over 16)
- any compensation paid will not benefit the offender in any way. This can be harder to show than you think! Get advice before claiming.

The CICA publishes a special leaflet on child abuse.

How do I make a claim?

Claims for compensation are made to the Criminal Injuries Compensation Authority, Tay House, 300 Bath Street, Glasgow G2 4JR Tel: 0141 331 2726. You can write or telephone for an application form, a copy of the tariff, and a guide to making a claim. There are also special guides available on getting compensation for loss of wages or earning capacity as well as on appeals.

When filling out the form, remember:

- some injuries will only be compensated if you got medical attention
- claim the right tariff – for example, if your burns are moderate rather than minor, it's worth £2,500 more
- make sure you claim for all your injuries, if more than one
- This is an extract from *Victims of Violent Crime*, written for Legal Services Agency Ltd by Simon Collins, Advocate, and Paul Brown, Principal Solicitor at LSA.

© *Legal Services Agency*

How ChildLine helps children

Your questions answered

Q: What is ChildLine?
A: ChildLine is the only free national helpline for children in Britain. It was launched in 1986 by Esther Rantzen who acts as its chairman.

Q: What does ChildLine do?
A: The charity provides a confidential counselling service for any child with any problem, 24 hours a day, every day.

Q: What sorts of things do children ring about?
A: Physical and sexual abuse are the two largest single problems that children call ChildLine about. But children also call about a wide range of other problems, from studying to family problems.

Q: How many children use the service?
A: Around 10,000 children try to call ChildLine every day, but lack of funds means that only about 3,000 of these calls can be answered.

Q: What happens when a child contacts ChildLine?
A: ChildLine's trained counsellors listen to children, and comfort, advise and protect them.

Q: What can they do for children in danger of abuse or violence?
A: With the child's consent, ChildLine can act directly to protect children in danger, by linking up with the emergency services and statutory authorities such as social services.

Q: What other practical help can they offer?
A: ChildLine can refer children to other appropriate sources of help for specific problems such as pregnancy, drug abuse or HIV/AIDS.

Q: What does ChildLine do for the children's welfare in general?
A: ChildLine gives children a voice – using its unique access to children's views and experiences to let decision-makers know what children think. ChildLine can also focus public attention on issues affecting children's welfare and rights.

Q: Is telephone the only way to contact ChildLine?
A: Children can write to ChildLine using its freepost address if they feel unable to call – every letter is answered by a counsellor, taking care not to place the child in any danger by doing so.

Q: Are counsellors paid for their work?
A: ChildLine counsellors are volunteers and all know that their contribution of time and commitment may have helped change the lives of children they have spoken to.

Q: How is ChildLine funded?
A: ChildLine is an independent registered charity, and is dependent on the support of the public and of business to maintain and expand its unique service for children.
Please remember, for thousands of children, ChildLine is a lifeline, a vital source of help and protection.

- The above information is from ChildLine. See page 39 for address details.

© *ChildLine*

Row over child abuse claim

NSPCC argues that the problem affects one in six children but should all sexual offences, from rape to 'flashing', be grouped together?

Relations between the Government and the National Society for the Prevention of Cruelty to Children, Britain's leading children's charity, were last night under strain after a day of recriminations over NSPCC figures on the extent of child sexual abuse.

Other child welfare experts joined the Department of Health's criticism of the society's survey findings that almost one in six adults claims to have suffered sexual 'interference' as a child.

Michele Elliott, director of Kidscape, a group which campaigns on children's safety, said on BBC radio: 'I think it is rubbish to put out a report that says that one in six adults has been sexually abused as a child – in fact, it is dangerous and it is highly irresponsible.

'It trivialises the issue of child sexual abuse and it detracts from those children who have been seriously abused.'

Allan Levy, QC, a leading expert on child law who co-chaired the inquiry into the so-called pin-down regime in Staffordshire children's homes' said: 'I think some of the definition, or lack of definition, in the subject-matter makes me rather cautious and also makes me think that there may be an element of exaggeration.'

The criticism centres on the way that the NSPCC survey, conducted by Research Surveys of Great Britain among a sample of 1,032 adults, drew no distinction between the 4 per cent of people who said they had been raped, the 11 per cent who said they had been molested and the 10 per cent who said men had indecently exposed themselves to them.

John Bowis, junior health minister, has said the findings are 'headline-grabbing' and 'risk crying wolf'. But the NSPCC is standing by

By David Brindle, Social Services Correspondent

the research and its decision to publish it.

Christopher Brown, the society's director, told a press conference yesterday: 'I find it very odd that a government minister can trivialise research which people find important to them.'

Some other experts rallied to the NSPCC's cause. Gerrison Lansdowne, director of the Children's Rights Development Unit, said a narrow definition of abuse denied children's rights.

The force of Mr Bowis's reaction, however, reflects the sensitivity of the Health Department on the child abuse issue ahead of publication next Wednesday of research expected to signal a

fundamental shift in child protection work.

Ministers and officials plan to use the research to call for a greater concentration on supporting children at risk, and their families, and less stress on the search for criminal evidence of abuse. The department's fear is that they will be accused of neglecting abuse.

In this context, the timing of release of the society's findings – even though they are by no means out of line with some previous studies – is regarded in Whitehall as unhelpful

The NSPCC did in fact yesterday come out in support of a change of emphasis in child protection work 'The primary objective of the system must be to respect the child's right to protection, but to do this in a way which is just and enables many disadvantaged families to receive the help they need,' the society said.

Victim

'I would have been in my late forties before I came to terms with what had happened to me'

To Ernest Woollett, any form of sexual interference can constitute serious and damaging abuse – if the victim has nobody to turn to, writes David Brindle.

Although the abuse he suffered took place more than half a century ago, he still talks graphically about the scars. At the time, he was seven, a wartime evacuee living away from his family. 'I cried when it happened and was ashamed I had been a coward. I would have been in my late forties or fifties before I came to terms with what had happened to me,' says Mr Woollett, now 62.

The abuse, which he is reluctant to describe but which he calls very serious, took place twice. He says the abuser was a teacher. 'For many years I had this idea of running him over. I became very much a loner, not trusting anybody, extremely aggressive. I couldn't form any close relationships.'

Although he married and had two children, he worked away from home as a welder in the construction industry and drank heavily. The marriage ended after 27 years.

It was the counselling that Mr Woollett and his former wife underwent to try to save the marriage that led him to face up to what he had suffered as a child. He is now a trained counsellor with Survivors, a group which helps men who have been sexually abused. 'I have worked with hundreds of survivors and what I have learned is that you cannot define seriousness in terms of abuse,' says Mr Woollett, of east London.

'If there is a child who has somebody who indecently exposes themselves to them and that child is so terrified by the experience that they cannot deal with it and cannot go to their parents and explain what has happened then that can create tremendous problems.

'If, on the other hand, a child can go home and say: "Mum, this dirty old man in the park has just done all these things to me", and can actually talk it through with their parents, there is much less chance of that being a long-term problem.'

Ernest is now a trained counsellor with Survivors, a group which helps men who have been sexually abused

---

Victim

'I felt like damaged goods, dirty. I was disgusted with myself'
As told to Sally Weale

From the age of five, Judith Smith (not her real name) was sexually abused by her stepfather. The abuse was regular – two or three times a week – and continued until she left the family home when she was 16.

It was full penetrative sex, even in the early years. Her mother would go out to work in the evening, and Judith would sit in the lounge and wait for her stepfather to come home.

Listening for his car to pull up outside, she almost wished he would hurry up so it would all be over. Once at home, he would take her to the bathroom where he would wash her, like a ritual. Then he would have sex with her.

At first he kept her quiet by threatening that she would be taken away from her mother if she told anyone. Later, as a teenager, he threatened her with physical violence. Judith never told a soul.

At 16, she left the family home in Hastings, East Sussex, and placed herself in care. There was a police

investigation but no charges were ever pressed as there was no corroborating evidence. Her mother, she feels, subconsciously knew what was going on, but in the end stuck up for her husband rather than her daughter.

For a long time after she left home Judith, now 31 and married, suffered from depression. She was withdrawn and isolated, terrified of men and full of self-loathing. 'I felt like damaged goods. I was disgusted by myself. I felt dirty and untouchable.'

Fifteen years after she walked out of the family home – after attending countless therapy and support groups – she still goes for weekly counselling to deal with the aftermath of her experience.

Like junior health minister John Bowis, who has criticised the NSPCC report, Judith disagrees with lumping together statistics on sexual interference in childhood, taking into account everything from a one-off incident of indecent exposure to long-term sexual abuse.

'Although being flashed at can be traumatic depending on the circumstances, there's probably a lot of people for whom that sort of thing would be a huge joke. It's not the same thing at all.'

In her experience, victims of sexual abuse tend to minimise their ordeal. It was only after group therapy when she had the experiences of others with which to compare her own that she realised quite how seriously she had been abused.

'I've learned to accept that the abuse happened and that it was and is a part of my life. For good or for bad, that was how it was and I can't change it.

'People generally think of sexual abuse just as a single act, rather than the long-term consequences and emotional impact it has on somebody.

'I don't have the same anger I had when I left home. I can't say I forgive him. All I can do is live with what happened and accept myself, and accept it as part of my life without being ashamed of it.'

Speaking out about abuse

What every young person should know

What is child abuse?

Abuse occurs when adults hurt children or young people under 18, either physically or in some other way. Usually the adult is someone the child or young person knows well, such as a parent, relative or friend of the family. There are four main kinds of abuse:

- Physical abuse includes hitting, kicking and punching, and may even lead to death.
- Emotional abuse includes sarcasm, degrading punishments, threats and not giving love and affection, which can undermine a young person's confidence.
- Neglect occurs when basic needs, such as food, warmth and medical care, are not met. Being thrown out of home may also be an example of neglect.
- Sexual abuse occurs if an adult pressurises or forces a young person to take part in any kind of sexual activity. This can include kissing, touching the young person's genitals or breasts, intercourse or oral sex. If an adult asks you to touch his or her genitals, or to look at pornographic magazines or videos, these are also examples of sexual abuse.

As well as causing suffering at the time, there may be long-term difficulties for young people who have been abused. All forms of abuse are wrong and have damaging effects on children and young people.

Not getting your own way all the time is not an example of child abuse.

Why does it happen?

No one knows exactly why some adults take advantage of their position of authority over young people in this way. There may be many different reasons. Stress, money problems, unhappy circumstances, the feeling of having no power in adult relationships, and having been abused as a child may all play a part. But it is hard to predict with certainty which factors cause an adult to abuse a child.

Some adults may even convince themselves that there is nothing wrong with their behaviour, or that it is for the child's own good.

But whatever the reason, abuse is always wrong and it is never the young person's fault.

Dear Anita . . .

Anita Naik, Problem Columnist in *Just Seventeen* magazine, answers some questions.

No one understands

Please help me. I'm 15 years old and will be taking my GCSEs this year. My problem is that I can't concentrate on anything because I feel so unhappy and depressed. I just want to hide myself away and cry most of the time, but I don't know why. My mum never really listens to me. She just doesn't want to know about my problems and keeps telling me not to be so stupid. I can't talk to my mates about it because they think I'm weird.

Gary, aged 15, Nottingham

Don't despair Gary. You're certainly not weird – or alone! Lots of people feel depressed without knowing exactly why – especially during adolescence. With exams looming and important decisions to make about your future, this is bound to be a stressful time for you. The best solution is to talk through your worries with an adult you trust. If your parents won't listen, then try talking to a close relative or a sympathetic teacher at school. You may find it easier to talk to someone on a helpline. You can ring ChildLine or the NSPCC Child Protection Helpline (see *Are you all right?* overleaf).

I feel dirty

I just don't know what to do. I'm 14 and my dad is making me have sex with him. Sometimes I feel angry and confused, and at other times I feel dirty and ashamed. I want to tell my mum but I'm afraid that she won't believe me. Please, please help me. I'm really desperate. I feel very confused because in some ways I love my dad, and I don't want him to go to prison. I just want the abuse to stop.

Anne, aged 14, Birmingham

Photo: NSPCC / Naomi Schillinger. Posed by model

I understand how bad you must be feeling. Remember, you are not to blame in any way for what has happened to you. Please tell your mum what has been going on, as soon as you can. If you feel you can't tell your mum, or you try and she doesn't believe you, then tell another adult you trust. You may find it helpful to talk to ChildLine or the NSPCC Child Protection Helpline (see *Are you all right?* on this page). You will probably need help to overcome your experiences. Your dad won't necessarily be sent to prison, though he will need help to understand that what he has done is wrong. In time, you may well be able to rebuild your relationship with him.

They make my life hell
I used to like school, up until a few months ago. There's a gang of three girls in the fifth form who've started to pick on me and they're making my life hell. Every time I see them they ask me to lend them money. If I say I don't have any, they start pushing me around and calling me names (I'm quite small). And it seems to be just me they pick on. Should I tell my teacher, or will that make things worse?

Corrine, aged 12, London

I know how cruel and upsetting this kind of bullying can be, and these girls need to be stopped. It's easy to be tough when there are three of you against one. Do you have friends who would help you confront these girls in public? Tell the bullies what cowards they are, and that you will tell their teacher what is going on unless they stop their threats. If you feel you can't do this, then you should tell your parents or the adult you live with, and ask your teacher for help right away. Most teachers are used to handling this sort of problem and should be able to stop these girls without making it difficult for you. You may also wish to ring ChildLine who receive many calls about bullying (see *Are you all right?* on this page).

I feel ashamed
About two years ago when my mum was in hospital, a good friend of my mum and dad used to come round to look after me until dad got home from work. I've never told anyone this before, but he used to bring round girlie magazines and get me to look at them with him. He said it was normal for boys my age to do this. Once he made me touch his penis and tried to touch mine. He told me to keep it a special secret. I can't keep this secret any more, I feel ashamed about what happened, but don't know what to do.

Tim, aged 13, Devon

It's not you who should feel ashamed. By showing you pornographic pictures and asking you to touch his penis, this so-called 'friend' committed sexual abuse, which is a criminal offence. He betrayed your parents' trust and took advantage of you. He asked you to keep it a secret so that he wouldn't be caught. I suggest you tell your parents or someone you trust exactly what you've told me. If they don't believe you, please don't give up, but keep telling another trusted adult until someone does. I realise this may not be easy, especially as the abuser is a family friend. This man may be abusing someone else, so he must be stopped – now. There are free helplines that offer support and advice for young people who have been abused. You can ring ChildLine or the NSPCC Child Protection Helpline (see *Are you all right?* on this page). Or your parents may want

to contact the social services or the NSPCC for help (see *What happens next?* opposite).

Protect yourself
If you have to walk alone after dark, choose a busy, well-lit route. And never take short cuts through parks or secluded areas.

Trust your instincts about people you meet. If you're in doubt, don't go off with them, particularly if you will be alone.

If someone attacks you in any way, it is OK to shout, kick, bite and do anything that will help you to escape.

If anyone tries to pressurise you into sexual activity, or wants to make you do things which do not feel right, you have a right to tell them not to – even if the person is someone you know and love.

Are you all right?
If you think that you are being abused, or you have feelings or difficulties which you think may be related to having been abused when you were younger, please talk to an adult you trust, or ring a helpline.

Talk to an adult
It is almost impossible for a young person to stop abuse or recover from it without involving an adult. Try and find the words to tell an adult you trust what is happening. If you can't find the words, try writing

something down and practise saying it, or ask a friend to help. If the adult you tell doesn't believe you, keep telling until someone does.

Ring a helpline
You can call either of the helplines below free of charge, at any time of the day or night. You can call from any phone, including a public telephone. If you can't get through straight away, please keep trying. Helplines can also help you work out who to tell and how to tell them, and can put you in touch with organisations which can help you.

NSPCC Child Protection Helpline
Telephone: 0800 800 500.
This helpline is for young people and children as well as parents and other adults. You can ring if you think you are being abused yourself, or if you are worried about a friend or any other young person or child. The NSPCC will offer advice and take any necessary action to stop the abuse.

ChildLine – Telephone: 0800 1111
This helpline is for young people and children, and can help with any kind of problem, including abuse. You can also ring them if you are worried that a friend is being abused. If you don't want to phone you can write to them at: Freepost 1111, London N1 0BR. You do not need a stamp.

Kidscape – Telephone: 0171 730 3300
You can ring Kidscape for information on how you can beat bullying. A special bullying counsellor is available on Tuesdays and Wednesdays, between 9.30am and 4.30pm. Or write for a free leaflet, enclosing a SAE, to 152 Buckingham Palace Road, London SW1W 9TR.

What happens next

When you tell an adult about serious abuse, he or she may have to involve other people to help you sort things out. Usually there will be a social worker, and sometimes a police officer and doctor. What happens next is called an 'investigation'. In order to help you, these professionals will ask you questions to find out exactly what happened. These

Is that a fact?

Try our quiz below. Cover the answers, and for each question, choose whether you think the statement is true or false. Check your answers and see how well you did.

1. When a young person is abused, the offender is usually a stranger.

False. The abuser is a total stranger in only one in every six or seven reported cases of abuse of young people and children.

2. Young people are always taken into care if abuse is suspected.

False. Young people are taken away from their families in only a very small number of cases, when it is thought dangerous for them to stay at home. Most return home, just as soon as it is felt they will be safe.

3. Abuse only happens in poor families.

False. Child abuse can happen in any kind of family.

4. The NSPCC helps adults, as well as young people and children.

True. The NSPCC gives counselling to adults who were abused as children, or who are in danger of abusing their own children.

5. Abusing very young children is not that bad, because the children won't remember much about it when they are grown up.

False. People who were abused when they were very young may not remember exactly what happened to them, but they may well experience emotional and psychological problems during their teens and adult life.
© NSPCC

questions may be embarrassing or difficult. But the adults involved are used to talking to young people who have had similar experiences, and should make it as easy as possible for you. As part of the investigation, the professionals will probably also speak to your family and other people who know you well. After the investigation there may be a 'case conference' where the professionals will meet and make decisions about how best to help you. You might be able to go along to all or part of the case conference.

During the investigation and case conference, it is important that you make sure that the professionals know how *you* feel. Try not to be afraid to ask questions, and let them know how they could make things easier for you.

Young people who have been abused are only taken away from

home if it is felt that it is dangerous for them to stay. The majority stay in their own home. Most of those who are removed return home just as soon as it is felt that they will be safe.

If you would like to find out more about investigations and case conferences, and how to cope with them, please write to the NSPCC for a copy of their booklet called *Child abuse investigations: A guide for children and young people.*

● This article has been published as part of the NSPCC's public education campaign activities. It is designed for young people aged 12-16 years, but may also be suitable for some young adults. If you would like more copies, or would like a copy of the leaflet *Happy children, sad children* which is aimed at 8-11-year-olds, please contact the NSPCC at the address on page 39.
© NSPCC

Church wants law eased to help child prostitutes

Charity urges protection rather than prosecution

By Sarah Boseley

A two-year campaign for the decriminalisation of child prostitution is being launched today by the Church of England charity, the Children's Society, which is calling for protection rather than prosecution for young people on the streets.

Child prostitution is child abuse, says the society. In a report on ways to help children who sell themselves, published today, it calls for the offences of soliciting and loitering to be removed from the statute book for people under 18. Ian Sparks, chief executive of the society, said: 'This is not a quick and dirty one-off to get some publicity and then move on.

'We have been working with young people on the streets for 10 years and this is part of our continuing campaign.'

Advertising posters will carry the slogan 'A man has sex with a 10-year-old prostitute. Who do you think should pay for it?'

The proposals will be controversial, and not only with the political Right. While the National Society for the Prevention of Cruelty to Children backed the campaign, the Association of Directors of Social Services gave a cool response.

Their spokesman, Bill Hendley, social services director for Coventry, said decriminalisation 'could very easily be exploited by pimps and others, leading to many more under-age children being led into prostitution than is currently the case'.

The law in many cases offered protection 'for vulnerable and often severely abused children against the predatory behaviour of some very ruthless men and women'. But the society argues that 'most current responses do not treat child prostitution as exploitation. The response of treating children and young people as offenders encourages pimps, clients, the media, the public – and young people themselves – to view them as such'.

Young people on the game risk violence, sexual harassment and rape, says the report. But if they see themselves as offenders, they are unlikely to go to the police for help.

The society believes no child willingly becomes a prostitute. 'Prostitution is very often a survival strategy for young people on the streets who have no money, food or shelter,' said Mr Sparks. 'We know from our practical experience that many have already been abused at home and have low self-esteem.' Home Office figures show that between 1989 and 1993, nearly 1,500 young people under 18 were convicted for offences relating to prostitution and a further

1,800 were cautioned.

The numbers are rising. Cautions of girls aged 10 to 16 rose by nearly 50 per cent and convictions by 10 per cent over the period.

Often police pick up the children only to return them to the family or residential home from which they have run away. The majority have been in children's homes.

Channel 4's *Dispatches* programme tonight will claim some staff know that children are on the game, but fail to help them.

The game's up: redefining child prostitution. Available from the Children's Society, Edward Rudolf House, Margery Street, London WC1X 0JL.

Case study 1

Abuse victim asked for help many times, but received none

Hannah's family broke up because of sexual abuse when she was eight. She always maintained that being put into care was punishment for having been abused.

By the age of 12, she had run away several times from her residential home, angry that nobody was listening to her and frustrated at not being placed in a foster home. By the time she was 14, she was absconding frequently and experimenting with drugs.

After her fathers' death, she became a frequent solvent user, explaining that it blocked out the hurt.

Under the influence of friends on the streets, she started to get involved in sexual activities for money, food, shelter and affection. When things got too much for her she would cut her arms with broken glass. One evening she was arrested for soliciting and received a conditional discharge.

She says she was bullied at school and in the residential home.

She asked for help on many occasions, but none was forthcoming. Her behaviour grew worse.

Hannah now lives in a hostel, with no job and no GCSEs. She has always said she would like to work with children but has been told that with soliciting on her record, she will not be able to do so.

Case study 2

The runaway who became terrified of pimp's violence

Sally was severely bullied in her children's home. She ran away, aged 12, and sought refuge with a Children's Society project eight times in five months of 1993. She had also been trying to harm herself.

She spent the next six months in a secure unit because of social workers' concerns that she might kill herself. During the following six months, she was in and out of residential placements and a refuge, or sleeping rough.

On the streets, she became involved with people in the sex industry. She told refuge workers that she was terrified of violence from the man she called her boyfriend if she did not meet him at arranged times.

She spoke of the first time she had been taken to the red-light area and put to work. She saw nothing of the money that was exchanged.

She said she felt the only way to break with the people controlling her would be through placement in a secure unit. She usually arrived at the refuge early in the morning, exhausted and hungry, and would sleep all day before disappearing in the early evening. She has made no contact with the refuge since January.

© The Guardian
October, 1995

A crusade for the victims of tourism

A Dublin-born priest based in the Philippines is seeking legislation to allow for 'sex tourism' offenders to be prosecuted in their own jurisdictions

By Lorna Siggins

Murder, financial misconduct, drug dealing, are all extra-ditable offences, yet there is little international recognition of the scale of child abuse within the 'sex tourism' trade.

This is according to the Philippines-based Irish Columban priest, Father Shay Cullen.

The Government should introduce legislation which allows for the prosecution of such offenders within their own jurisdiction, Father Cullen said in Dublin yesterday.

One Irish teacher is facing prosecution for offences committed in Asia following surveillance by the Australian police federation and Interpol, he said.

The Columban, who has campaigned on behalf of street children and prostitutes in the Philippines for over 20 years, said offenders should be prosecuted in the first instance within the jurisdiction where crimes were alleged to have been committed. 'In so many cases, these people have fled. That's where extradition, or trial within their own jurisdiction, has to come in.'

Reports of two other Irishmen involved in such offences have been relayed to his organisation, the Preda Foundation, based in the Philippine port of Olongapo.

The Government there has begun to take a hard line on prostitution and the sex trade, and Father Cullen has been asked by the President, Mr Fidel Ramos, to serve on a committee for the special protection of children.

Originally from Glasthule, Co. Dublin, Father Cullen has been in the Philippines for 26 years and founded the Preda Foundation. It campaigned successfully for the closure of US naval bases and was involved in filing a case on behalf of 6,800 children who were not receiving financial support from American fathers.

The Preda Foundation also campaigned on behalf of some 8,000 HIV-positive cases in Olangapo, which it blamed on the US military presence. The statistics were disputed by the US Government. Unicef estimates that there are an estimated 60,000 child prostitutes trapped in a form of slavery in the Philippines.

New legislation introduced by the Philippine Government is not being enforced, however, and the Preda Foundation has to gather much of the evidence in many of the legal cases, he said. The 17 full-time staff – 'We do not take volunteers' – employed by the foundation are involved in prevention programmes, economic projects for women and children, and reintegration programmes. Two Fianna Fail TDs, Mr John O'Donoghue and Mr Eoin Ryan, introduced a private members' bill the Sexual Offences (Jurisdiction) Bill, in June.

According to Mr O'Donoghue, the party's justice spokesman, it 'aims to extend the criminal law of the State to try sexual offences against children committed elsewhere which, if committed in Ireland, would be considered a crime'. Father Cullen said he would meet Mr Ryan this weekend and he had received considerable support for a similar campaign in Britain. The Garda had also expressed an interest in consulting him on international co-operation, he said.

© The Irish Times
November, 1995

'More than 5,000 young girls are prostitutes'

By Glenda Cooper

More than 5,000 under-age girls are working as prostitutes in Britain, and the number caught soliciting has doubled since 1990, according to a three-month investigation.

Girls aged under 16 were found not only in London but in red-light districts of cities such as Cardiff, Southampton, Manchester, Doncaster and Leeds, and in one case a 12-year-old was caught soliciting.

Recently the focus has been on so-called 'sex tourists' who travel abroad, but according to Rob Kiener, who carried out the study for *Reader's Digest*, there are a growing number of juveniles who sell themselves at home.

Mr Kiener said children in care and runaways are the most vulnerable. But 'it's not just some lower class or underclass. There was a girl in Doncaster, 14, living at home, who met her pimp in a bar she had gone to with her brother. Her mum was a hospital physiotherapist.'

Although social workers may suspect a girl in care is prostituting herself, by law they cannot physically restrain her. And if the police pick her up they must take her back to social services. Often she can be back on the street within hours.

A spokeswoman for the Children's Society, which will launch a national campaign on child prostitution next month, said: 'Locking children up isn't an adequate response to the problem of prostitution. But they need to be protected and secure accommodation is an option.'

Young girls are frequently lured in through what they see as affection or love. Often starved of attention in their life, they are showered with gifts, clothes and drugs until their 'boyfriend/pimp' demands a return on his investment.

When 14-year-old Cassie's pimp believed she was withholding money he burned her breasts and nipples with a lighted cigarette, then he and three friends gang-raped her 'to teach her a lesson'. And in Cardiff three pimps armed with knives, metal bars and a samurai sword forced four teenage girls, the youngest 14, to work as prostitutes. Each night the girls were strip-searched for their earnings which amounted to more than £1,000 a week.

> **They are showered with gifts, clothes and drugs until their 'boyfriend/pimp' demands a return on his investment**

Even after physical abuse many girls do not leave. 'It's like a battered wife who can't leave her husband,' said Mr Kiener. 'They say things like

"he only beats me because he loves me".'

'Jane' (not her real name) a project worker doing prostitute outreach in West Yorkshire, agreed. 'It's a case of "better the devil you know". If they leave they lose their friends, where they live and their income,' she said. It angers her that it is the girls rather than the pimps or punters who tend to end up with a criminal record.

One solution has been found in Nottingham, after the anti-vice squad found they had arrested twice as many juveniles for soliciting in 1992 as in the previous year. Closer liaison with local authority and social services has meant, since 1992, nearly 100 pimps have been convicted.

One success was the case of Oswald 'Lucky' Golding, who had been suspected for some time. Social workers tipped the police off that a man fitting his description was hanging round a home where two girls, aged 13 and 15, were regularly absconding. The police kept Golding under surveillance, and he was convicted, receiving a two-year jail sentence.

'We took an extremely close look at the girls involved and found many of them were in care,' said Inspector Dave Dawson, of Nottingham Police. 'Many were being forced or intimidated by individual adults to come on the streets. So we targeted the areas where the liaison was formed.'

Last year Doncaster police were told that a 12-year-old was soliciting. They found her several nights later offering herself for £20. After local media coverage, the town's older prostitutes reported an influx of kerb-crawlers asking 'if they could get them a 12-year-old girl'.

What's wrong with a good smack?

. . .it didn't do me any harm . . . surely children need discipline

Surely a little smack on the legs doesn't count?

Yes, it does. If hitting children is wrong, then the difference between 'a little smack' and a beating is simply one of degree. Such questions show a lack of respect for children. In any case, 'little smacks' all too often lead to harder and more frequent ones. That's because hitting doesn't work except to relieve parents' feelings. If you let yourself smack your toddler for fiddling with the TV, what can you do when the toddler fiddles again except smack him again, harder? And what can you do with the five-year-old who refuses to stay in his room to cool off except lock the door . . ?

Surely you need to use physical force to keep children safe?

There is all the difference in the world between using your strength to snatch a child away from the hot stove, or prevent one from running into a busy road, and intentionally causing pain as punishment.

But is the ordinary kind of smacking that goes on in loving homes worth all this fuss?

Yes, it is – because violence really does breed violence , and violence is a major problem today. We are not saying that hitting at home is the only cause of that violence, but we are saying – with a lot of evidence to back us up – that ending hitting at home would help to reduce it.

Children model much of their behaviour on their parents. Parent who use physical punishment are directly teaching their children that physical force is an acceptable way to sort out problems. If we want less violent adults we have to bring up children who believe that physical force is not acceptable.

How can you expect parents under stress, suffering from family poverty, etc, not to hit their children?

Of course our society needs to do far more for those who bear the burden of child-rearing, and EPOCH will support those campaigning for reforms. But there are no clear links between such social factors and the frequency or severity of hitting children. There is plenty of evidence that ending physical punishment will help to reduce family stress.

In any case, why should children and only children wait for equal protection from this sort of violence until we have sorted out all these major social ills?

But children need effective discipline, don't they?

Parents who smack take the effectiveness of physical punishment for granted because it serves to interrupt tiresome behaviour with tears and to vent parental frustration. The interruption and the relief are temporary, though. Physical punishment does not produce better-behaved children. Parents who start smacking when their children are babies are just as likely as other parents to smack frequently as the children get older. Physical punishment does not work as a 'final sanction' or 'last resort' either. Until caning was banned in state-supported schools, their own punishment books showed that it was the same handful of pupils who received corporal punishment again and again.

To be effective, a disciplinary technique must do two complementary things: it must set external limits on children's behaviour so as to keep them safe and acceptable to their parents and others, and it must help them to develop the self-discipline that will gradually replace those external controls with the internal controls we call 'conscience'. Physical punishments do neither. They cannot show children where the limits are because they are only smacked or beaten when those limits have already been overstepped. They cannot help in the development of self-discipline because they only tell children that they have done wrong; they neither describe the crime nor suggest the preferable alternative.

Learning how to behave is exactly like other kinds of learning in that it depends on children understanding what is wanted of them; being motivated to co-operate and make efforts, and being set a good example. Children who are hit often misunderstand the cause of the punishment. Many spankings are the result of cumulative parental stress in which one last small misdemeanour is one too many. The child sees the parental anger but relates it only to that last event and believes he was hit for 'spilling my drink' or, more accurately 'because you were cross'. Premeditated punishment for carefully explained reasons fares no better: the hurt, anger and humiliation caused by the punish-ment deafens children to the reasons for it. And even if the reason is understood, those feelings leave no room for remorse or determination to do better.

And in the longer term, physical punishment actually works against children's development of socialised self-control because it denies them a parental model for it. Parents who hit their children set them an example of the very opposite: of the efficacy and acceptability of larger people imposing their will on smaller ones by brute force.

● The above is an extract from *Hitting people is wrong – and children are people too*, produced by EPOCH. See page 39 for address details.

© EPOCH

When it is right to smack

A report published this week opposes smacking. Anne Davis, a child-minder who won a legal battle against a council for the right to smack, makes her case

A healthy family life is the basis on which the community depends and, in turn, the well-being of the whole nation. And every healthy family understands its responsibility for bringing up children.

I gave up a career in teaching to become a professional mother. As far as my own children are concerned, I am the expert.

So before any of us are misled into attaching the slightest importance to the Gulbenkian Foundation's report, *Children and violence* – and, in particular, to its utterly predictable opposition to smacking – we should examine carefully the people who produced it.

When we hear that a 'commission' is to investigate and report on a subject, most of us would assume that has been appointed by some official body. This so-called commission was entirely self-appointed and almost every member supports EPOCH (End Physical Punishment of Children) or has run an organisation which has signed EPOCH's charter.

The chairman, Sir William Utting, assured me that he had no such allegiance and was entirely independent. But when researchers from Families for Discipline (for whom I act as spokesman) investigated this claim, they found his name on the list of EPOCH's individual sponsors compiled in October 1993.

And even the Gulbenkian Foundation itself turns out to be the second-largest financial contributor to Approach (Association for the Protection of All Children), which is the charity attached to EPOCH – providing it with more than £60,000 between 1991 and 1994. The whole set-up is so lacking in objectivity that it makes my blood boil. When such spurious 'commissions' set out to reach the conclusion upon which they have already decided before they begin, they invariably use the phrase 'all the evidence suggests that . . .' What they really mean is 'all the evidence which we could find to prove what we wanted it to prove'.

Some time ago Dr Robert Lazarlere, a psychologist attached to Kansas State University, tested children's reactions and responses to different corrective techniques by assessing how long it was before the same antisocial offence was repeated. He found that a combination of reasoning followed up, if necessary, by a smack had a longer-lasting effect than reasoning alone or smacking alone. There was no mention of that evidence in the Gulbenkian report.

You cannot legislate for what happens in the home and no natural parent would ever dream of hurting a child. Smacking children was prohibited by law in Sweden in 1979 and in the 16 years since that Act of Parliament the rate of reported non-accidental injury to children has remained the same.

When the law is invoked there is a very real danger that parents become afraid to follow their best instincts. They fear that if their child gets a smack and tells a friend or teacher, they will have the social services knocking on their door. There are reports of parents in Sweden who have so lost their confidence in determining what they can or cannot do to control a difficult child that they have voluntarily handed over that child to the social services. If that is true, it is one of the saddest things I have ever encountered.

I was married in 1986 and when the first of our three daughters was born I decided I wanted to be at home to look after her. My husband, who is a computer-draughtsman, could not earn quite enough on his own so I became a registered child-minder. By the time I qualified, our second daughter was a year old and I found having another child of about the same age in the house was very good for her.

Before I started minding this child his mother said that she had to

Ken Pyne

WE'RE AGAINST PHYSICAL PUNISHMENT BUT UNFORTUNATELY HE ISN'T

smack him occasionally. She would allow me to do the same if I felt it was appropriate – provided she was told about it at the end of the same day. This was entirely right and exactly what I would have demanded if in her place.

That was why I refused to give a verbal undertaking to Sutton Borough Council never to smack a child in my care, and that was how I came to be struck off its list. When I was told I would be deregistered, I appealed to the magistrates' court and won. The Sutton social services appealed against the magistrate's decision (backed by EPOCH, among others) and so we progressed to the High Court.

Just because I, and all the other parents who now actively support Families for Discipline, believe that a quick smack is sometimes appropriate, it does not mean that we ever regard it as a first option or,

indeed, as a regular one. It should be used only when a child is deliberately and repeatedly defiant or has deliberately hurt another child.

If you tell children to do something, or not do something, then the child must understand that there are certain rules and penalties for disregarding your orders. And if a child has been hurt by another and sees nothing happen apart from a ticking-off and an instruction not to do it again, then that child is left with a sense of injustice.

The purpose of imposing discipline is the development of self-discipline. If you give children a reason for an instruction, it gives them an option – either to be a good child or to receive the penalty.

Whether smacking is the correct punishment or not depends partly on its motive. If it is done to relieve the frustration of the adult then it is neither effective nor appropriate. It

must only be used for the good of the child – not to hurt but to teach a respect for the rules.

We all have rules and we obey them for two reasons – either because we agree with them or because we are afraid of the penalty if we disregard them.

Little children do not necessarily have the ability to agree or disagree but they need to be made aware that there are penalties for breaking those rules. For a very young child any penalty must be immediate. And when a child needs to be disciplined it is vital to encourage a child to say sorry and then to have a cuddle. This cuddle demonstrates that it was the behaviour that was unacceptable, not the child that is unloved.

The best judges of how to bring up a young child are the parents who know and love that child better than any expert. *© The Telegraph plc London, 1995*

Smacking is wrong and doesn't help discipline

Smacking has to be wrong because we all agree that hitting people is wrong and children are people – aren't they?

When a bigger child hits a smaller one in the playground, to get his sweets or his turn, we call him a bully . . .

When a youth hits an old lady to get her handbag, we call him a mugger . . .

When a parent hits a child to make him or her obey, is it really any different?

Maybe you will say it is different because that parent's motive is good. She smacks her child 'for good reason'; maybe even 'she does it for the child's sake'. But our society doesn't accept that 'good motives' can make hitting people right. A policeman who hits a suspect behaves wrongly, however keen he may be to solve a crime.

Maybe you will say that smacking children is different because it's in the family and

therefore part of a relationship which is both loving and stressful. But that would make it perfectly all right for your partner to end arguments with you by giving you a good smack. And that isn't all right at all. If your partner did that he'd be called a 'wife-beater'.

Under British law, parents (and other carers) can hit children as much as they like, short of doing them serious injury, but hitting anyone else is a criminal assault.

If any smacking is wrong, all smacking must be wrong. Lots of parents agree that hitting children and causing real pain is wrong but believe that what they do doesn't because 'I only give a little tap'

Of course there are degrees of wrongness. It's worse to murder someone than to mug her and worse to thrash a child with a belt than to smack with your hand. But that doesn't make the 'little tap' all right because it isn't the degree of pain

that makes the difference, it's inflicting any pain (or 'sting' or 'smart') on purpose. Every parent will sometimes have to grab a child at the edge of the road or snatch a small hand before it can touch the iron. Sometimes that kind of safety-action will hurt a child and lead to tears. But it wasn't meant to hurt, it was meant to prevent hurt.

One mother said 'Don't talk about hitting and pain. You're making an ordinary smack sound cruel and horrible on purpose . . .' But when her two-year-old played her up while we were talking she smacked him and she chose his bare legs rather than his nappy-padded bottom. She did hurt him on purpose and it was horrible.

• The above is an extract from *Smacking – a short-cut to nowhere*, produced by EPOCH. See page 39 for address details.

© EPOCH

Report attacked over call to stop hitting children

The Gulbenkian Foundation's report on *Children & Violence* – disclosed in the *Daily Telegraph* last month – was published yesterday. Its opposition to smacking was swiftly criticised, writes Celia Hall

A national charter of non-violence was proposed yesterday in a 300-page report which covers child abuse, playground bullying, armed robbery and boxing.

The report, *Children and violence*, comes from a commission convened by the Gulbenkian Foundation in the wake of the murder of two-year-old James Bulger by two boys.

But it was immediately condemned by those who defend the rights of parents and carers to discipline children by smacking.

Sir William Utting, former Government Chief Social Worker and Chief Inspector of Social Services at the Department of Health, was chairman of the commission.

He said yesterday: 'Hitting people is wrong. Hitting children teaches them that violence is the most effective means of getting your own way.

'We must develop a culture which disapproves of all forms of violence. All the lessons of my working life point to the fact that violence breeds misery. It does not resolve it.'

But Anne Davis, the child-minder at the centre of a controversial court case two years ago, accused the commission of bias.

Mrs Davis, who is now the spokesman of Families for Discipline, said: 'Half the organisations represented are children's rights activists. They did not ask the opinions of people with different views.'

Mrs Davis won the right to smack in a legal battle against Sutton Borough Council. She had refused to sign a form undertaking not to use any physical discipline on children.

Children and violence, which drew together 17 professionals involved in children's protection and rights issues, fitted with the decision of the social welfare unit of the Gulbenkian Foundation to accept the United Nations Convention on the Rights of the Child.

This asserts children's rights to protection against all forms of physical or mental violence. All six of the children's organisations represented on the commission support the aim of ending by education and legal reform all physical punishment.

Earlier yesterday, Lord Jakobovits, former Chief Rabbi, told Radio 4's *Today* programme that the report had missed an essential point. 'I do not find in the summary of the report a single reference to the word discipline,' he said.

He said that to speak only of a child's rights without adding the duties of obligation and responsibility distorted the moral sense of children.

Referring to Proverbs, Lord Jakobovits said: 'We are told the man who spares the rod hates his son.'

Robert Lynn, former professor of psychology at the University of

Ulster, now director of the Ulster Institute for Social Research, said the commission was guilty of either ignorance or ideology. He supported Mrs Davis in her legal fight.

'They have selected people committed to a particular point of view,' he said. 'Children differ in their ability to learn right from wrong just as they differ in intelligence. On the whole, middle-class children tend to learn more easily. A raised voice may be all that is needed.

'Children born into the underclass may not learn so easily. A smack may be necessary. Children learn about discipline through fear. It is a recipe for failure to undermine society's ability to teach children through fear.'

Peter Newell, a member and research co-ordinator of the commission who is co-ordinator of EPOCH, End Physical Punishment of Children, said that since 1989, when his organisation began, 60 organisations had joined its campaign.

These organisations include the National Society for the Prevention of Cruelty to Children, the National Children's Bureau and Save the Children. 'This is no longer a minority view. All the major children's charities now support these aims,' he said.

In its 'commitment to non-violence in parenting, child care and education', the commission gives suggestions by which adults can re-appraise their behaviour towards children. It says that adults must make it clear to children that all interpersonal violence is disapproved of on principle.

Respecting children within the family

Families need to recognise that children are people in their own right, and not the property of adults who have responsibility for them. Building the relationships between adults and children on the following principles will lead to more open and sharing family life.

Think child friendly

International Year of the Family highlighted the importance of families in children's lives. The quality of relationships children experience within their families will have a crucial impact on their present and future lives.

Children have the right to:

- Recognition of their value as people now and not merely as adults-inwaiting

- Receive physical and emotional care

- Feel safe from all forms of physical and mental violence and deliberate humiliation, including physical punishment from parents

- Express their views on all matters of concern to them and have them taken seriously

- Respect for their evolving capacity, including the gradual acceptance of responsibility and decision-making

- Information appropriate to their age both to encourage participation in and to help them understand decisions that affect their lives

- Respect for their privacy

- Respect for their religious and other beliefs.

These principles are enshrined in the UN Convention on the Rights of the Child. In December 1991, the UK Government formally agreed to abide by them.

Think child friendly

These questions might help you think about and develop your relationships with the children you care for.

Valuing children as people now
Could you do more to promote children's sense of self-worth? How do you help them prepare for adult life while at the same time getting the most out of each stage of their childhood?

Physical and emotional care
What do you do to make sure that children have sufficient care and protection without losing the right to be adventurous and develop independence? What levels of risk do you feel are appropriate for children?

Safety from violence
If children are to learn respect for themselves and others, they must be respected by the adults caring for them. All forms of physical punishment and deliberate humiliation are degrading. What can you do to develop alternative, positive approaches which encourage children to behave?

Children are people in their own right, and not the property of adults who have responsibility for them

---

Listening to children and taking them seriously
How do you ensure that children take part in decisions within the family? Do you encourage children to be involved in decisions that affect them? How willing are you to take their decisions seriously?

Respecting evolving capacity
Children's ability to take responsibility for certain decisions will be considerably helped by encouragement and support from their parents. How do you step back from a protective role, and begin to allow your children to take responsibility for their own actions?

Information
Information is essential for children to develop their understanding and have the confidence to participate in decision-making. How do you ensure that your children have information appropriate to their age or understanding?

Respecting privacy
Privacy and respect for confidentiality are important for children of all ages, but take on increasing significance as children grow older. Do you respect their wish for privacy in relation to their own bodies, their belongings and their friendships?

Respecting beliefs
Parents have responsibilities to provide moral guidance to their children. How do you provide children with the necessary information and guidance they need to help them form their own opinions and beliefs without exerting undue influence?

© *United Nations International Year of the Family*

31

Bullying – why it matters

From Young Minds Information Service

What is bullying?

Bullying can take many forms. It is not only being physically aggressive. Any kind of aggression that is intended to hurt someone else can be bullying. This includes calling other children nasty names, teasing or spreading unpleasant stories about them, as well as pushing, threatening, hitting and kicking. Of course, most children are called names sometimes, and not all teasing is nasty. Many children, especially boys, also get into fights every now and then. But if a child is repeatedly singled out by another or by a group and finds it difficult to stand up for themselves, then he or she is being bullied.

Is bullying normal?

Many children get involved in bullying at some time during their school-days – they may be bullied themselves, they may bully someone else, or they may see a friend being bullied. Bullying can be especially common in primary school. In fact, most children behave aggressively sometimes, but it is only a minority of children who become regular bullies. Like all children, they need to learn that it is unfair and wrong to bully others.

Why do children bully?

Children can bully for all sorts of reasons. Most likely they bully simply because they see nothing wrong with it. They don't understand or care how much it hurts to be bullied, or they think the bullied child deserves it. For some other children, bullying may be a sign that they are troubled or anxious about something. They may be unhappy at home, or they may be being bullied themselves. Or they may be finding the pressure of school-life difficult to cope with. Some may hurt others to avoid being hurt themselves.

Boys and girls can often bully in different ways

Name-calling and teasing are the most common types of bullying, but a lot of boys also use their physical strength to bully others. Girls are more likely to rely on excluding someone from a group or spreading hurtful stories about them. This can be just as upsetting. The important thing to remember is that any form of bullying can be very worrying for the child being bullied.

Does bullying matter?

It can sometimes be difficult for adults to understand the distress and misery bullying causes, especially if the bullying is 'only' teasing or name-calling. But being persistently teased or called names, like any other kind of bullying, can make children very unhappy. It can seriously interfere with their school-work, and they may even not want to go to school. Being picked on can mean children develop a low opinion of themselves. Anyone who is bullied for a long time may even come to believe that they deserve it and that there is something wrong with them. Being bullied regularly can be associated with problems later on in life as well. Some adults who were bullied as children find they often get depressed, lack self-confidence and feel resentful.

Bullying matters also to bullies. Some may feel isolated and ashamed of the damage they cause. They may even come to believe they are bad and worthy only of punishment.

There is also evidence that aggressive behaviour which is not effectively challenged in childhood can sometimes carry on into adult life, leading to violence and crime.

What can be done?

Schools can do a lot to stop bullying happening in the first place. Research shows that when everyone involved with the school – teachers, pupils, parents, and non-teaching staff – takes a strong and open stand against bullying, it is far less common. It must be made clear that all pupils have a right not to be bullied. It is especially important that schools encourage pupils to accept that it is not wrong to 'tell'. But children also need to know that something will be done to stop the bullying. A list of organisations that can help teachers and schools deal with bullying is below. There are also groups that can provide advice and support for parents, and phone numbers for children themselves to ring if they are involved in bullying.

Children who have been badly bullied may be helped to regain self-confidence and assert themselves better through counselling or psychotherapy. Children who bully

others may be less easy to help if they do not think they have a problem. Some, however, may be frightened by what they do and can also benefit from counselling. *Young Minds* can tell you about what children's mental health professionals do and where to find help locally.

Where to get help

Help for parents and teachers
Anti-Bullying Campaign
10 Borough High Street
London, SE1 9QQ
Tel: 0171 378 1446
The Anti-Bullying Campaign provide a support service for the

parents of bullied children and produce fact sheets and guidelines for teachers. They also run regional support services.

Kidscape
152 Buckingham Palace Road
London, SW1W 9TR
Tel: 0171 730 3300
Kidscape is a registered charity which provides books, videos, teaching packs and leaflets on how to deal with bullying. They also operate Parents' Bullying Helpline on Mondays and Wednesdays, 9.00am – 5.00pm. Send a large SAE for free 20-page booklet 'Stop Bullying'.

The Scottish Council for Research in Education (SCRE)
15 St Johns Street
Edinburgh, EH8 8JR
Tel: 0131 557 2944
SCRE have produced a pack – 'Supporting schools against bullying: the second SCRE anti-bullying pack' (cost £10) – to help schools involve the whole community in taking action. One booklet included in the pack – 'Bullying and How to Fight It' (cost £3.25) – is for families and is also available separately

© Young Minds

Most pupils 'bullied by age of 12'

By John Carvel, Education Editor

Most children have suffered bullying by the age of 12, and a minority as early as three or four, according to research published yesterday by the Centre for Consumer Education at John Moores University in Liverpool.

The bullies usually became active while at primary school, operating in groups of two or three. They were more likely to make other children frightened by threats and insults than by hitting, scratching, stealing or hair-pulling.

Anne Miller, the centre's director, said the results ran counter to academics' previous assumptions

that bullying mostly started when children entered secondary school.

She established that 1,444 of the 2,741 boys and girls questioned in their early years at 10 secondary schools in North-west England said they had been victims of bullying.

For most of the victims, the problem started between the ages of 9 and 11 and usually it was stopped after the intervention of a teacher, parent or friend.

But 6 per cent of the victims said the problem started before their fifth birthday.

'Males tended to bully males and females to bully females.

'For both sexes it was more likely that they would be bullied by a mixed group than by a member of the opposite sex,' the survey said.

Most victims said the bullying lasted for less than a month (52 per cent) or less than a year (27 per cent), but 17 per cent said it lasted for more than a year and 5 per cent said it lasted more than five years.

© The Guardian
October, 1995

Home win

**After repeated bullying at school Edward Upton took drastic action –
he left. Now, after studying at home, he has 12 GCSEs**

By Roisin McAuley

When Edward Upton went for his GCSE English language oral he thought it would be like a French oral, and the examiners would chat to him in English. Hardly a problem.

'But the first thing they asked me was "What are your two prepared speeches?" I thought "What?" I was completely unprepared. I had two minutes to think about it and then I made speeches about polo and home education.' He got a B.

Edward knows a lot about home education. In the late spring of 1993, when he was 13, he decided to leave the public school where he'd been unhappy and teach himself at home. He now has 12 GCSEs – an A*, 3 As and 7 Bs – all achieved through correspondence courses and home-study guides.

'I was picked on at school, and by one boy in particular. Whenever I walked past he'd say "jelly belly" or "You're so fat".'

The bully made Edward's life miserable at prep school. His father had died in a car smash when Edward was three. He was bullied about not having a father as well as about being overweight. The first year was the most miserable. But then Edward found a group of friends and the protective power of the peer group. He also enjoyed learning how to study efficiently.

'We had life skills classes. I was taught that most people can only concentrate for 40 minutes, so I'd fully immerse myself for only 40 minutes at a time.'

It was a lesson which stood him in good stead when he found out that the prep-school bully went to the same public school. Here, Edward felt more isolated. 'You get a ringleader like him and the rest of the group copy his actions. If you're different you're picked on. I'm academic. I've never really enjoyed football, rugby, cricket. I never felt part of the school.' His housemaster was very sporty 'and a bit of a bully himself', says Edward.

So Edward left after one and a half terms. He went to the library and looked up the law on staying at home. 'It appeared it was the responsibility of parents to see that children get a suitable education.' Edward's mother, Rosemary, was very supportive. She had taught Edward and his younger sister at home when they were aged seven and five and couldn't settle at school. But this was more complicated.

She spent a lot of time on the telephone trying to find out where Edward could sit his GCSEs if he studied at home. Then there was the problem of finding a correspondence course. 'You can't look around a correspondence course like a school. We saw advertisements and sent for brochures and we liked the look of the National Extension College (NEC).' It charged £150 per subject – with a discount for more than eight subjects. Edward took eight subjects with the NEC. For French and Latin he had home tutors. For physics and geography he used Letts Study Guides. 'I had a system whereby I'd study for four hours in the morning. The secret is mixing up. I'd read for 30 minutes and then I'd watch the Open University programmes on TV. They were better than the GCSE ones.'

Edward found the examination board system more hassle than studying for or sitting the exams. 'I'd ring up the examination board and get referred from department to department. You couldn't be an external candidate in every subject with the same board. So we had to swap and shop around.'

'Edward's case is unusual and probably unique,' says Robert Leach, Director of the Cambridge-based NEC. 'We cater very much for adult returners. They usually do no more than five subjects. He would have had to work very hard and send off several assignments a week. I'm very impressed.'

Edward's best mark was an A* in physics which he did completely on his own with the Letts Study Guide. 'I've not had anybody to my knowledge do that before,' says the Physics Guide's author Michael Shepherd. 'Everything you need to get a good grade is in the book, but you need to be pretty dedicated.'

'It was just what suited him,' says Rosemary Upton. 'He was very well taught at prep school and that stood him in good stead. He needed to catch up with himself and digest life. He's the philosophical sort.'

The hardest thing was criticism from friends and relatives. 'They thought I was mad.' Men, and especially male relatives, thought it would be very bad for Edward 'cooped up at home with his mother'. But he had a lot of outside influences staying at home. 'We had a lot of support from the community.'

Edward has won a bursary to Millfield, where he is now a weekly boarder. 'I've really enjoyed my first weeks. It's gone better than I thought. I did feel I'd get better grades at school. But doing the exams at home has made me feel I've achieved something quite big. I'm already to go out into the world and get on with my work.'

How to beat bullying

Why do they do it? Is there any excuse for bullying behaviour? Read on and find out what makes a bully tick . . .

Peer-pressure bullies

They're scared

There are always bullies who roam around in gangs and there are always those on the sidelines who do lots of dirty work for the ringleader.

They're probably being bullied too, because they don't want to stand up to the bully for fear of being singled out for attention. In other words, being just as nasty as their 'friend' makes for an easier life.

Do they mean any harm?

They may seem uncomfortable with what other members of the group are doing and may even try to apologise to their victims when the main bullies aren't around.

Insecure bullies

They put on a show

When you're not sure whether people like you, the temptation's there to show off a bit. Some people try to be funny, others may wear their best clothes to school, but there are always going to be those who bully because they think it'll make them look impressive.

They're sarcastic and cruel

Insecure people want to make their friends look up and take notice, so intimidating other people is an easy way to go about it. They'll pick on those least likely to answer back or to pose any threat and probably stick to making cruel jokes at their victim's expense.

They're looking for approval

They're desperate for the go-ahead from their mates, so will always be looking to them for a reaction to everything they do. If there's no audience around they'll probably leave you alone.

Bullies with their own problems

They're in trouble at school

Lots of bullies are involved in a spot of bother when it comes to other areas of their school lives. The people they pick on act as a sort of diversion or something to take their minds off other problems or maybe they just have a hard reputation they want to live up to.

They're used to bullying

Older brothers and sisters (or even parents) may have been violent or nasty towards them all their life, and to them it's natural to get rid of their own anger by taking it out on others.

They don't like themselves

Some bullies are so troubled that they are probably disruptive and violent in other areas of life too, perhaps at a youth club or at school. If this is the case, then they'll no doubt be well known to teachers and parents who may have already had complaints from other people.

Boyfriend bullies

Are you being forced into a sexual relationship or are you frightened by your boyfriend's aggressive behaviour? Then you must . . .

Talk

It may be that he doesn't realise his behaviour is intimidating you. Talk to him and make it clear how you expect to be treated.

Listen

Does he have problems he's not letting you in on? Find out if he feels pressurised by friends to act a certain way when he's with you.

Think

Is it worth sticking around? Remember – being harassed or touched up is a form of bullying, even if the culprit is your boyfriend.

A bully writes . . .

Dear Mizz,

I always read your magazine and I hope you don't mind me writing to you. I saw a piece you did on bullying and thought I'd write to get something off my chest.

I am disgusted to say that I was once a bully. I spat and swore at people and even beat a girl up so badly that I broke her arm. I'm 19 now and have never been ashamed to admit that I deeply regret the things I've done in the past.

Peer pressure and the fact that my own father used to sexually abuse me and beat me up made me very depressed when I was younger. I couldn't hit back at my dad, so I took it out on other people. I'm glad to say that I left home at 17 and have never hit or even sworn at anyone since. I'd like to apologise to anyone I hurt, and I want you to know that if I could turn back time I would be a nicer child.

My message to people who are being bullied is to stand up for yourself and ask the bully what their problem is. If someone had stood up to me or even asked why I bullied them I would probably have told them about my dad. Who knows? We may have ended up being friends.

From an ex-bully, Dorset

Celebrity comment

'Bullies want to be feared, but you've got to realise that often they're upset about their own lives and so they feel the need to upset other people too. Feel sorry for them, but don't be trodden on.' – *Scott Bradley*

● The above is an extract from a special report which appeared in *Mizz*, called 'How to beat Bullying'.

© *Mizz*

What can you do to help?

Perhaps you've not a victim, but would like to do something to help another person who's being bullied. We've got some tips for you if you've had enough of standing on the sidelines . . .

A friend in need

You may want to pretend that nothing's happening and turn a blind eye because . . .

- You don't want to make trouble for yourself. If the bullies have made your mate's life a misery, what's to stop them doing the same to you?
- Your friend may not want your help. He/she probably thinks it's not a problem that anyone else can help them solve.
- You may feel that the bully will only get his/her friends involved if you intervene and things will get even more out of hand.
- Your friend hasn't confided in you that he/she's having problems and you don't want to seem like you're poking your nose in.
- You don't want to lose friends. It may be that the bully is also a mate of yours and you feel it's best not to take sides.
- Your friend may have sworn you to secrecy, so you'd be betraying that confidence if you got help from somewhere else.

How can you help?

Everyone can do something to help, even if you don't know the victim (or bullies) well. Quite often the person in trouble will insist that he/she can handle the situation on his/her own, but if you think things are getting serious then you might want to take action anyway. Here are some tips if you think it's time for the bullying to stop . . .

Let a teacher know

Don't feel as though you're grassing – all you're doing is making your concern known to someone in a better position to help. You don't necessarily have to name the bully, just mention in passing that you've noticed the victim is getting a bit of hassle. If the teacher keeps an eye on him/her it will probably become apparent who the culprits are and most schools have tried and tested policies on how to deal with bullies. NB: If the bullying isn't happening at school then try to talk to an adult who knows both the bully and the victim. He/she could be a youth club leader, employer or an adult friend of both parties.

Listen to the victim

He/she may not even be a friend of yours, but it will always help them to know there's someone there who is willing to talk about the problem and give support. Don't be afraid to introduce yourself – admitting to someone else there's a problem may be his/her first step to getting help.

Be a friend

Bullying is a very lonely experience, and victims may feel that they don't fit in with the crowd because they've been singled out for attention. Give the victim's confidence a boost by asking him/her along next time a gang of you go out together.

Take what they say seriously

If someone takes you into their confidence and admits they're having problems with the bullies, it's really important that you're sympathetic. Don't laugh it off and say 'It's nothing' or 'Just forget about it'.

Let them know about ChildLine

He/she can ring the usual ChildLine number on 0800-1111 and it won't cost anything to call. Why not suggest he/she phones from your house (the call won't show on itemised phone bills) or say you'll go with them to a phone box?

Never join in

You may even dislike the person you know is being abused, but bullying is not something that anyone deserves. Think about the victims you know and ask yourself if what's happening to them is fair. How scared would you feel if you were in their position? It may be easier to join in with the bullies than stick up for the victim, but if you can't bring yourself to help them please don't make the problem worse.

Photo: Larry Bray / ChildLine. Posed by model.

'I was physically and verbally bullied for four years on the bus to and from school. Eventually the bus route was changed and I no longer saw the girl who was making my life a misery, but I'm sure that if it hadn't, then the abuse would have continued. I didn't want to tell anyone because I was scared of what would happen, but I wish now that I'd done something about it. If you know someone who's being bullied then please offer your help. Convince them to tell someone about what's happening, or ask if they'd prefer you to say something. You don't have to mention who's doing the bullying, just say you've noticed your friend is getting a bit of hassle and hopefully the teacher, or whoever, will take it from there. Someone's got to get the ball rolling, even if the victim won't speak out for him or herself. I only wish someone had done the same for me.'

Lisa Smith, Sheffield

Celebrity comment

Bad Boys Inc.
Ally: 'I was bullied and I know it's difficult, but my advice is to hold your head up high and stand up to them.'
David: 'Try to ignore them, it's always the bullies who have the real problems, not the victims.'
Tony: 'Bullies will look back on what they did and regret it a lot as they get older.'
● The above is an extract from a special report which appeared in *Mizz*, called 'How to beat Bullying'.

© *Mizz*

Hard lessons

It is not only children who threaten children in school. Here, Judy Darby, a former pupil, tells a disturbing story of bullying from a different quarter

We hear all the time about my age-group being a problem to schools. Perhaps we are, but it's not all one-sided. As teachers get weighed down with an increasing amount of paperwork they get impatient and less inclined to explain the difficult bits. They shout or use sarcasm

Don't they realise how humiliating that is? Have they forgotten the sheer hell of being shown up in front of your mates?

Take me, for example. Primary school was good. It was safe and friendly and I did well. Then I settled in quite quickly at secondary school; I was very quiet and didn't know many people. The problems with my work didn't really start until the end of my second year.

I tried explaining this and even asked to be moved to a lower group. But the more I asked for help, the more I heard the same answer: 'No, you're not stupid, of course you can do the work!'

The teachers started humiliating me in front of the whole class by telling everyone that I got the lowest marks.

I was constantly in detention for not completing any work, but what they would not understand was that I wanted to learn. I just needed some help.

I started to truant. At first I would just miss a few lessons, but then it was weeks, even months, and if I did go to school I just caused trouble. It was just my way of coping. The teachers were making it hard for me, so I would make it hard for them. I would disrupt the whole class. Afterwards I felt guilty, but still believed they deserved it.

I would be told things like: 'Why do you bother coming to this school? We don't want you here!' It's terrible to feel unwanted.

After a year they sent me to a tuition centre. I learnt so much and I enjoyed it. But my six weeks ended and it was time to go back to school.

It took me a month to find the courage to go back. I still did not receive the help I needed. After two months I was expelled, this time through no fault of my own. I took the blame for something I had not done. And no matter how many times I tried telling them it wasn't me, they wouldn't listen.

I'm not trying to say that teachers don't get it rough because they do. But so do the students. A teacher's job is to teach, not just expect us to be able to do every piece of work put in front of us.

© *The Guardian*
July, 1995

INDEX

ADDITIONAL RESOURCES

You might like to contact the following organisations for further information. Due to the increasing cost of postage, many organisations cannot respond to enquiries unless they receive a stamped, addressed envelope.

Calouste Gulbenkian Foundation
98 Portland Place
London
W1N 4ET
Tel: 0171 636 5313
Fax: 0171 637 3421
Charity dealing with social welfare and education issues. Funds research and the publication of reports on their findings. Ask for their publications list.

Child Poverty Action Group (CPAG)
1-5 Bath Street
London, EC1V 9PY
Tel: 0171 253 3406
Fax: 0171 490 0561
Promotes action for the relief of poverty among children and families with children. Publish *Poverty* magazine.

ChildLine
2nd Floor Royal Mail Building
Studd Street
London, N1 0QW
Tel: 0171 239 1000 (admin)
Fax: 0171 239 1001
ChildLine is the free, national helpline for children and young people in trouble or danger. It provides confidential phone counselling service for any child with any problem 24 hours a day. Produces publications. Children or young people can phone or write free of charge about problems of any kind.
Write to:
ChildLine
Freepost 1111
London, N1 0BR
or telephone:
Freephone 0800 1111

Children's Legal Centre
c/o Law Department
University of Essex
Wivenhoe Park
Colchester
Essex, CO4 3SQ
Tel: 01206 873 820
Produces publications.

EPOCH (End all Physical Punishment of Children)
77 Holloway Road
London, N7 8JZ
Tel: 0171 700 0627
Aims to end the physical punishment of children. Produce literature on a variety of issues relating to physical punishment.

Legal Services Agency
134 Fenrew Street
Glasgow, G3 6ST
Tel: 0141 353 3354

National Children's Bureau
8 Wakely Street
London, EC1V 7QE
Tel: 0171 843 6000
Fax: 071 278 9512
Provides information on children's needs in the family, school and society. They publish a series of factsheets called *Highlights*, including one on the subject of bullying and another which covers child prostitution.

National Society for the Prevention of Cruelty to Children (NSPCC)
National Centre
42 Curtain Road
London, EC2A 3NH
Tel: 0171 825 2500
Has a network of Child Protection Teams and projects to protect children from abuse. Can help parents, carers and relatives who feel they may be in danger of harming their children.
Operates the Child Protection Helpline offering counselling and support. Tel: 0800 800 500.

Save the Children Fund
17 Grove Lane
London
SE5 8RD
Tel: 0171 703 5400
Fax: 0171 730 2278
Strive to promote the rights of children. Publishes a wide range of leaflets, booklets and reports.

Scottish Child Law Centre
4th Floor, Cranston House
108 Argyle Street
Glasgow G2 2BH
Tel: 0141 226 3434
Fax: 0141 226 3043
Gives advice, information and commentary on child law and children's rights for the benefit of under 18s in Scotland. Freephone for young people (in Scotland) 0800 317 500 (9am-5pm Monday to Friday)
Advice line for adults: Tel: 0141 226 3737 (10am-4pm Tuesday to Friday).
Business line: Tel: 0141 226 3434 to order publications, get information about training etc. Publishes leaflets, briefing papers, conference papers and other publications.

The Children's Society
Edward Rudolf House
Margery Street
London, WC1X 0JL
Tel: 0171 837 4299
Fax: 0171 837 0211
Works for children to be able to grow in their families and communities and change the conditions that stand in the way of their own lives.

The National Council for Family Proceedings
Centre for Socio-Legal Studies
University of Bristol
3 Priory Road
Bristol, BS8 1TX
Tel: 0117 928 8136
Fax: 0117 974 1299

Young Minds
102-108 Clerkenwell Road
London, EC1M 5SA
Tel: 0171 336 8445
Fax: 0171 336 8446
Young Minds, the national association for children's mental health. Produces a range of leaflets, reports, a magazine and newsletters.

ACKNOWLEDGEMENTS

The publisher is grateful for permission to reproduce the following material.

Chapter One: Children's Rights

The Rights of the Child, © HMSO Reproduced with the Kind Permission of Her Majesty's Stationery Office, January 1996, *The extent of violence involving children*, © Calouste Gulbenkian Foundation, *A guide to the Children's Act – for parents*, © The Council for Family Proceedings, *Youth rights in Scotland*, © Scottish Child Law Centre 1995, *At what age can I . . .?*, © The Children's Legal Centre, January 1996.

Chapter Two: Child abuse

If you care about children . . ., © NSPCC, *ChildLine logs 20,000 please for help a year*, © The Telegraph plc, London 1995, *Telling about child abuse*, © Scottish Child Law Centre, *Children's problems*, © ChildLine 1995, *Fact or fiction?*, © NSPCC, *ChildLine speaks out*, © ChildLine, November 1995, *Victims of violent crime*, © Legal Services Agency, *How ChildLine helps children*, © ChildLine, *Row over child abuse claim*, © The Guardian, June 1995, *Speaking out about child abuse*, © NSPCC, *Is that a fact?*, © NSPCC, *Church wants law eased to help child prostitutes*, © The Guardian, October 1995, *A crusade for the victims of tourism*, © The Irish Times, November 1995, *'More than 5,000 young girls are prostitutes'*, © The Independent, September 1995, *What's wrong with a good smack?*, ©

EPOCH, *When it is right to smack*, © The Telegraph plc, London 1995, *Smacking is wrong and doesn't help discipline*, © EPOCH, *Report attacked over call to stop hitting children*, © The Telegraph plc, London 1995, *Respecting children within the family*, © United Nations International Year of the Family.

Chapter Three: Bullying

Bullying – why it matters, © Young Minds, *Most pupils 'bullied by age of 12'*, © The Guardian, October 1995, *Home win*, © The Guardian, October 1995, *How to beat bullying*, © Mizz, *What can you do to help?*, © Mizz, *Hard lessons*, © The Guardian, July 1995.

Photographs and Illustrations

Pages 2, 19, 24: Anthony Haythornthwaite / Folio Collective, pages 4, 11: Katherine Fleming / Folio Collective, pages 6, 15, 32: Andrew Smith / Folio Collective, pages 7, 9, 28, 37: Ken Pyne, page 10: Sandra Lousada / NSPCC, pages 13, 16, 17, 36: Larry Bray / ChildLine, page 21: Naomi Schillinger / NSPCC, page 22: Duncan Ridgley / NSPCC.

Craig Donnellan
Cambridge
April, 1996